House Concert

House Concert

IGOR LEVIT
FLORIAN ZINNECKER

Translated by Shaun Whiteside

polity

Originally published in German as *Hauskonzert* © 2021 Carl Hanser Verlag GmbH & Co. KG, München

This English edition © 2023, Polity Press

The translation of this work was supported by a grant from the Goethe-Institut.

Polity Press
65 Bridge Street
Cambridge CB2 1UR, UK

Polity Press
111 River Street
Hoboken, NJ 07030, USA

ISBN-13: 978-1-5095-5355-6

A catalogue record for this book is available from the British Library.

Library of Congress Control Number: 2022935473

Typeset in 11 on 14pt Warnock Pro
by Fakenham Prepress Solutions, Fakenham, Norfolk NR21 8NL
Printed and bound in the UK by TJ International Limited

For further information on Polity, visit our website:
politybooks.com

to our families
and
our friends

Acknowledgements

Work on this book ran like a constant through a time of turbulence, some of which was at first unforeseeable. For that reason alone, the writing of the book itself was never without its challenges: there was hardly an event that didn't have to be repeatedly postponed, hardly a plan that didn't have to be scrapped and redrafted. If it hadn't been for the unshakeable conviction of a lot of people that it was a good idea to write this book right now, and if those people had not in their own way accompanied and encouraged the process of its making with trust, generosity, expert understanding and patience, both making it possible and helping to carry it along: we would never have made it.

These include first and foremost Maren Borchers-Fromageot, Henriette Gallus and Kristin Schuster, Simone Bode, Anselm Cybinski and Andreas Neubronner, Felix Broede, Georg Diez, Boris Fromageot, Philipp Nedel and Thorsten Schmidt, Moritz Müller-Wirth, Kilian Trorier, Marc Widmann and Bettina Tschaikowski, Kai-Uwe Diaz Philipp and Martina von Brüning, Stefan Arndt, Christian Möller, Andreas Morell and Carolin Pirich, Ulla Kalchmayr, Justus Wille and Charlotte Hartwig, with particular thanks to Jo Lendle, the editorial team and the rest of the crew at Hanser Verlag, Hanna Hesse, Christina Knecht and Kirsten Vogelsang, and most especially to Margie Oberle and Kasimir Straubert, Stephanie Bartsch and the late Ralf Oberle. Antonia Goldhammer, Christiane Lutz, Elena and Simon Levit, Karin and Peter Zinnecker, and very specially to Nora Zinnecker.

Warmest thanks to you all!
Igor Levit and Florian Zinnecker

If you understood everything I said, you'd be me.

Miles Davis

Berlin, a Saturday in December 2019. Igor Levit is tired, his right arm hurts; it mightn't be the best day to get started.

Two days ago he got back from a short tour with the Deutsche Kammerphilharmonie Bremen. Hamburg, Wiesbaden, Vienna, Bremen, seven performances in eight days. The Brahms Piano Concerto No. 1 four times, No. 2 three times. In the weeks before that he played for four evenings each the first half of his Beethoven sonata cycle in Hamburg and Lucerne, on two evenings four sonatas, on two five. And in between there was his inaugural concert as piano professor at the University of Music, Theatre and Media in Hanover. On the programme: a movement from a symphony by Gustav Mahler, after that a passacaglia by Ronald Stevenson, lasting an hour and a half. Enough repertoire for a whole year. Or for three pianists.

Perhaps it would be better to start a few days earlier; it would be easy to make him look good. Then Igor Levit would be sitting at the grand piano right now, pounding the conclusion of the first Brahms concerto into the keys, stormy, ardent, bursting with energy, and then: applause, cries of 'bravo', ovations.

That's how books about pianists begin.

And not on a gloomy Saturday morning in a packed café in Berlin-Mitte, where the only available seat is the one by the door.

But there's nothing to be done.

Levit is late, even though his apartment is only a few blocks away. He walks jacketless through the icy rain. Neither his manager nor his press agent know about this date, despite the fact that there is hardly anything in Igor Levit's life that they haven't authorized.

But he isn't here for professional reasons. He has some time off – two weeks – his first free days since September, and the next concert is on Boxing Day. 'It's possible that in those two weeks I'll work out that I need another twelve.'

He takes off his glasses and runs his hands over his face.

How was the tour with the guys from Bremen?
'Ok.'

He runs his hands over his face again.

'You know, piano concertos take it out of you. Much more than solo recitals. I love doing solo recitals. Then I have two hours on stage, and those two hours belong to me. I might mess it up. But it's still mine. With a piano concerto I've got maybe forty minutes, maybe even only twenty. I sit there and there's nothing I can do, I'm completely dependent on the energy of the orchestra. If the orchestra's right, it's good, and if not, it gets difficult. I know from the very first bars.'

He kneads his right shoulder and pulls a face.

What's up with your arm?
'It's ok.'

Right now, his left arm almost hurts more than his right; last night Igor knocked the funny bone in his left elbow, by accident and quite violently. His right arm has already been sore for a few days: too much Brahms, too much Beethoven, too much everything.

'If I had to go up on stage later on, no problem. But this morning I could barely brush my teeth.'

We'd actually met up to talk about something else.
More precisely: about one question in particular.

Levit is one of the best pianists of his generation, some say the best of the century, which is quite an unsophisticated judgement, and not one that he himself likes to hear. One music critic applied the superlative, but he's not keen on such descriptions. His press agent has the term 'pianist of the century' deleted from all his interviews.

Recently almost all the big newspapers discussed his complete recording of the Beethoven piano sonatas. A few weeks ago a there was a big profile about him in *Die Zeit* and now Alex Ross, the music critic of the *New Yorker*, is coming to do another big profile, and *Stern*'s working on a piece as well. Bayerischer Rundfunk is planning a Beethoven podcast with him, thirty-two episodes, one for every piano sonata. In September he was on the stage of the Thalia Theater in Hamburg talking to Wolfgang Schäuble about the German constitution, and recently he was a guest on Maybrit Illner's political talk show on the ZDF channel to discuss hate speech. Igor might well be among the best pianists of the century – he's certainly the most visible. And then there's his Twitter account.

All that's really missing is a book.
Haha.
But seriously.

Almost all the articles, interviews and podcasts are either about Igor Levit, the pianist who expresses political opinions. Or Igor Levit, the Twitter activist who also plays the piano. Mightn't it be time to talk about how the two things come together, how it began and where it's going, in short: why Igor Levit sounds the way he does?

Levit says nothing.

Kneads his shoulder.

Looks out of the window into the gloomy morning.

'Quite honestly? No idea. No idea how long I'll keep on doing it. How long I want to carry on.'

How long he wants to carry on what?

'It could be that it's because I'm exhausted. But right now, I really don't know.'

He kneads his shoulder again.

'It's not enough for me. I'm constantly travelling, I play concert after concert after concert, but once the concerts are over, I don't sit down, pat myself on the back and say: Gooooood concert! Gooooood concert! Instead, I immediately ask: What's next? I'm travelling about at the speed of light, because I'm always worried I won't have time.'

He rests his head against the wall and shuts his eyes. But only for a moment.

'You know, right now there's not that much at stake. What can happen? I can play the Waldstein Sonata in G major rather than C major, and at half-speed – who's going to stop me? Or the Moonlight Sonata two octaves higher and really fast. So? If I do that they can say I'm a dick. So? I can play badly at a concert, I can get lost, forget how it goes. What happens then? I might get booed, I might get a lousy review and the organizer won't have me back. Will that kill me? No. Will I starve to death? Nope. So what am I afraid of?

He goes on kneading.

'It's not enough for me. The piano isn't enough for me either, I'm constantly playing pieces that are really too big for the piano. Just wait there for a second, I've got to go to the toilet.'

He leaves his phone on the table, and his glasses too. Outside it starts snowing, thin, ugly and relentless. It's nearly midday and not really light.

'Let's have a go', he says when he comes back. What? 'The book. Let's do it. Except I can't really say what I'll be doing in a few months.'

All set.

Right: shouldn't we be on first-name terms?

'Sure', Igor says, 'I'm Igor.'

Then he looks at his phone, and says by way of farewell, 'Right, I'm off to bed.'

#

The journey itself starts before that.

Wednesday, 18 September 2019. Igor steps onto the stage in the grand hall of the Elbphilharmonie in Hamburg. On the programme: three Beethoven sonatas and then a fourth, No. 21 in C major Opus 53, the Waldstein Sonata. Igor calls it 'the most life-affirming piece of music I know.'

The hall is in darkness, Igor sits in the beam of three spotlights shining directly down on him from above. It was the author Roger Willemsen who said that happiness is rarely to be found in a pure C major chord, but the Waldstein Sonata is one of the exceptions, because it begins with fourteen pure C major chords, *allegro con brio*. They feel like a pleasant shower of rain, like unease at the start of something, butterflies in your stomach before you get going. Like pure happiness.

In the hands of many other pianists, the Waldstein Sonata sounds like a hurdle race where the only thing that counts is following all the instructions as precisely as possible and not stumbling. You can hear the rules through the music. Igor, on the other hand, sets the music free. He plunges into the first movement at such a breakneck tempo that you're afraid it's going to send him flying off course. The movement is composed speed, a pounding heart, vibration. So many notes, so many individual sounds in a single sonata movement is rare. You can feel the tempo. Only once does Beethoven allow the music to get slower. If you ask him why he plays so fast, Igor says simply: Because I can. And because it's what Beethoven demands.

In the second movement the music pauses, the lightness has made way for melancholy. Igor sets the chords down so that all the notes stand motionless like columns in space; the music sounds as if it was written not by Beethoven, but by the very old Franz Liszt: every note comes straight from eternity. There is no hint of a melody striving to get somewhere. The notes are a physical state; nothing moves. Everything is what it is.

The music sounds three-dimensional. But not because it's coming from different directions: the work itself is three-dimensional. The harmonies create planes and pillars, spaces and doors to the next room. There is light and darkness, there is colour and temperature – and then a voice comes into the room.

Igor isn't the kind of musician to retreat behind the work. He says: I'm playing this, I make the rules. Not only is he not shy of saying 'I' – he's saying it's the only way.

But it will still be a while before he finds out who he means when he says 'I'.

And then, in the middle of the night, the sun comes up again. Igor summons a melody and chases it through the sound traditions of different eras, even those that come after Beethoven. You can hear Liszt and Rachmaninov, Debussy and Glass, and soon the music also gets a beat – are you allowed to play it like that? Why not, Igor says. Without the pianist the piece wouldn't even exist now. The finale starts small, gets bigger and ends up cosmic, a melody gives rise to a world, and in the end everything ends in pure euphoria.

Igor, on the stage in the Elbphilharmonie, takes a bow.
Plays an encore.
Which piece is unimportant.

On the way home the music still echoes, as it often does after concerts, but this time each note seems to have left a small footprint and the notes as a whole a big one.

What, if you'll excuse me, was *that*?
From whose life was Igor telling stories? From his own? Or the audience's?
Where do the colours come from, the nuances, the power?

Why does the Waldstein Sonata, that piece of music that's a good 200 years old, so often sound merely exhausted, overplayed, *competent*? And today so natural – no, so self-evident, as if it couldn't be otherwise, as if Ludwig van Beethoven hadn't at some point written it all down, but as if it had always been there and had just become audible for the first time.

Might that be the whole mystery? Does Igor sound as interesting as he does because he doesn't just play a piece of music, but at the same time – with complete commitment, and a complete sense of risk – brings himself on stage?

Because this is unambiguously not about C major, four-four time, *allegro con brio*, main subject, second subject. This is about much more than that. If it didn't sound so platitudinous and pompous you might say: it's about everything.

And if the reflection of life in the music is so exciting: what must life itself be like?

Or is all the tension, all the power, in the music, and everything else is bleak and empty?

What would be left if you took piano playing away from someone who plays piano like that? Would it even be possible?

How does someone who plays like that come to terms with himself?

#

So this is the story. Igor Levit, 32, not fully stretched by being the pianist of the century and at the same time being completely exhausted by it. In search of an answer to the question and for months in search of the question itself: who am I and what am I supposed to be doing?

And now?

Usually biographies consist of an uninterrupted narrative of events in a life which create the impression that the life described is a sequence of causalities which feel just as logical and conclusive at the moment when they are experienced as they do in retrospect. It is the attempt to give a meaning to things, and some things only acquire a meaning in context.

But life doesn't consist only of events, but also of feelings, intimations, urgency, tedium, insecurity, good and bad luck. And above all of more questions than answers.

Such a book also never consists of the absolute truth, but only ever personal truth. Stories that are told over and over and that have got better with each telling, in which narrators can barely agree on time and place, they only agree that everything happened exactly like that.

One possibility would be to begin at the beginning, or, even better, before the beginning. Then one would have to tell the story of how in the late winter of 1987 Elena Levit walked to the conservatoire in Gorki morning after morning, and home again evening after evening, to the tiny flat in one of the low-rise estates, and how she always talked to Igor in her belly, even though she still had no idea that the child she was pregnant with was going to be a boy.

And one would also have to tell the story of how, before Igor was born, she dreamt she was sitting at a concert, and on the stage her son was playing Piano Concerto No. 2 Opus 18 in C minor by Sergei Rachmaninov. And 15 years later, in the

Maria Callas Competition in Athens, Elena Levit really is sitting in a concert hall while on the podium her son really is playing Rachmaninov's Piano Concerto No. 2 Opus 18 in C minor.

Stories like that. But do they help?

To understand why a pianist plays as he plays, thinks as he thinks and feels as he feels, do you need to start before the first note? Particularly when he himself can't even remember that first note?

That might be true of lots of others, but it doesn't apply to Igor. Igor Levit can only be understood in the context of the immediate present.

There's also a very different problem with the past – but more of that later.

So we decide to focus on a little bit of present for the book. On that day in December there's a lot to indicate that the coming year would be a suitable period of time. Because it is largely planned and easy to grasp.

Igor's concert dates have been arranged for the whole year. It's the year of the celebration of the 250th anniversary of Ludwig van Beethoven's birth. Igor is one of the most in-demand Beethoven interpreters on the market, so there's a lot going on. In early February he's supposed to moderate an edition of the ZDF culture magazine programme *Aspekte*. On 10 March, his thirty-third birthday, he's giving a concert with two Beethoven piano concertos in the Elbphilharmonie. In May he's playing a tour of the USA, with his solo debut at the Carnegie Hall in New York. Then, in August: three weeks of the Salzburg Festival, with the Beethoven sonatas.

So far, so good.

We agree to meet up in Salzburg; three weeks seem like a good framework for discussions about the book. Enough time to go into it in depth. We'd see what's happened by then.

We knew no better.

Most of the things that this book considers were unimaginable on that day in December. But it doesn't matter.

When you're telling a joke it's important to know the last sentence when you start the first one. This book is not a joke.

#

The simplest option for telling the story of Igor's life is at the same time the best known and the most impressive: Igor's success story.

Born in 1987 in Nizhni Novgorod, a city in the Soviet Union that was still called Gorki at the time. Moves to Germany at the age of eight, first to Dortmund, then Hanover. Studies at Hanover University of Music, Drama and Media. Graduates with the highest marks ever awarded by the institution. His debut CD of Beethoven's last five sonatas wins *BBC Music Magazine*'s Newcomer Prize and the Young Artist Prize of the Royal Philharmonic Society. This is followed by a recording of the partitas of Johann Sebastian Bach, an album with the set of variations on 'The People United Will Never Be Defeated!' by Frederic Rzewski as well as the Goldberg and Diabelli Variations. The album of variations wins Recording of the Year at the *Gramophone* 2016 Classical Music Awards. His complete recording of the Beethoven piano sonatas tops the classical music charts. He gives solo performances at the Salzburg

Festival, at the Lucerne Festival, at the Elbphilharmonie, at London's Wigmore Hall, at the Royal Concertgebouw in Amsterdam, the Vienna Musikverein and New York's Carnegie Hall. Apart from all that, he guests with internationally leading orchestras, including the Berlin Philharmonic, the Cleveland Orchestra, the Leipzig Gewandhaus Orchestra, the New York Philharmonic, the Bavarian Radio Symphony Orchestra and the Vienna Philharmonic.

He is a holder of the 2018 Gilmore Artist Award and 2018 Instrumentalist of the Year of the Royal Philharmonic Society. In the spring of 2019, Hanover University of Music gave him a professorship. For his political commitment he was awarded the 5th International Beethoven Prize in 2019, followed in 2020 by the Statue 'B' of the International Auschwitz Committee.

This biography is printed in the programmes for Igor's concerts, in the booklets for his CDs, on his website. Nothing here is exaggerated; every word is true. But, and in common with every other artist's biography: these words don't relate, explain or substantiate anything. They contain only the results, but not the journey there. Only the highs, none of the lows.

#

Obvious things first: Igor is a pianist. That in itself explains a lot.

A pianist lives by playing in front of an audience. He masters performances. He lives for them.
Performances without an audience are possible, but pointless; music not only needs someone to make it but also someone to hear it. A pianist needs an audience, he needs a counterpart, he isn't self-sufficient.

Not least because he has spent by far the largest part of his life alone with music.

From early childhood onwards pianists spend a very great deal of time alone with themselves at the instrument, in the practice room, on tours, on stage. Which doesn't necessarily mean that pianists are lonely; that only happens when they can't be alone in a good way.

Their life is played out in notes; they learn to mould them so that they can be anything: love, pain, longing, courage. And if they have put enough of themselves into the notes, their listeners find themselves in them too.

'I play my music with my biography, my experiences and thoughts on this particular day', Igor once said in an interview with *Der Tagesspiegel*. 'And the audience hears the music exactly the same, in their own way. It's a hugely intimate process. If I ever lose the utopia of the audience interpreting along with me on equal terms, I'll hang up my hat as a pianist.'

Pianists learn early on to be self-reliant. They can focus on a single subject for a very long time. They are accustomed, in every concert, in every recording, throughout the whole of their career, to carrying all ultimate responsibility on their own shoulders.

But that's not all. Igor can only lead the life he leads because he performs effectively. He can only perform effectively if he is disciplined. He lives in a system of rules and laws, most of them unwritten. And these rules are no different from any rules in music: you're allowed to break them at your own risk. But before you break them, you have to know what they are.

Playing the piano isn't hard, at least in terms of the fundamental principles. You press down a key and hear a note. And you immediately hear how different a note can sound according to how much power you put into striking the key.

That's exactly where it starts getting hard.

On a violin it's three years before you achieve the first note, and wind instruments are complicated too.

That's why the piano is so good for children. Each note is a success; music immediately sounds like music.

When asked why he actually plays the piano, Igor says: because he can't play any other instrument.

'The simplest explanation is probably: because I started at the age of three and have never stopped. I crawled to the piano all by myself, I can't remember doing it.'

Sometimes as an encore Igor plays a miniature by Dmitri Shostakovich – a scherzo, Opus 90b, the first part of the Dancing Dolls, a piano suite from 1952. 'My mother always used to play this waltz with her pupils. I heard it as a young child.' The right hand plays a simple melody in three-four time, the left a simple accompaniment. A piece more for two fingers than two hands, any piano pupil could play it with a bit of practice.
The beginning, at least. After the middle part the melody stays in three-four time, while the accompaniment switches to four-four, and for sixteen bars the two run along in parallel, while the audience's synapses tie themselves up in knots. When playing too.
Too much is happening at the same time.

At least according to the criteria of people who aren't Igor. Too much at the same time has never been a category for Igor.

\#

One of the crucial evenings in Igor's career is 17 September 2004, a Friday. Igor, 17 years old, performs in the Piano Olympics in Bad Kissingen. A competition that is only open to participants who have already won prizes elsewhere. Other performers include: Martin Stadtfeld, who by this time already has a recording contract with Sony Music, and Alice Sara Ott, whom Igor knows from Salzburg, from the summer academies of his teacher Karl-Heinz Kämmerling. Igor plays Schumann, Beethoven and the Bach transcriptions of Max Reger, an unusual programme for a competition.

And he makes the acquaintance of probably two of the most powerful women in the German music business: Eleonore Büning, music critic of the *Frankfurter Allgemeine Zeitung*, and Kari Kahl-Wolfsjäger who, before founding the competition, established the KunstFest Weimar, runs the Beethoven Festival in Bonn and in 1986 came up with the Kissinger Summer, three not insignificant festivals in the German-speaking world.

He takes second prize. Like all prize-winners he's allowed to play in the Kissinger Summer the following year and, as part of the deal, also gets a series of other performance opportunities: for musicians a chance to collect routines, for the organizers of the competition the opportunity to write off their expenses.

Then a lot of time passes.

Early in 2010 Kari Kahl-Wolfsjäger called Igor and asked if he would like to join her on a trip to China. There was a cultural exchange between the Chinese province of Shandong and the state of Bavaria, which was sending a selection of young artists to China for International Music Week: several pianists, several violinists, some singers, for seven concerts over twelve days, in various configurations. Igor agreed. By now he was about to sit for his concert diploma, but otherwise he hadn't got much on his plate. He discussed two or three possible programmes and booked the fights to Beijing.

Igor travelled a day ahead, because he wanted to eat Peking duck, and some other musicians from the group flew out in advance as well. After landing, he saw an announcement on the monitors at the airport that the volcano Eyjafjallajökull had erupted in Iceland. A few hours later, because of ash at high altitudes, the whole of Russian airspace was closed. Air traffic was suspended across large parts of Europe, and a lot of his colleagues were stuck in Germany; the only pianist in the group who made it to China was Igor.

'Then, with giddy recklessness, I said: I'll take on all the concerts, what's the problem? In cities with a million people and no proper concert halls, it was quite an adventurous idea. I just played three times as many. I also had to dig out a whole lot of repertoire because we sometimes put on two concerts in one city – and I couldn't play the same thing twice.'

Igor played chamber music, accompanied Lieder evenings and violin sonatas, and also took over his colleagues' piano recitals.

'He knew all the works, and if he didn't, he'd learned them within a day', the music critic Eleonore Büning says in a radio interview with WDR. She was also in China – Büning had been with the Bavarian Radio Symphony Orchestra on a tour of Asia and wished she was back at home. But now she couldn't get away – and visited her old friend Kari Kahl-Wolfsjäger, who was rehearsing in Jinan with her troupe.

The conditions weren't ideal. On the stage of the conference centre in Jinan there was a grand piano that sounded as if it had been left in the garden all winter. Igor accompanied Mozart violin sonatas and Schubert Lieder, and finished with the Waldstein Sonata.

Eleonore Büning came into the hall in the middle of the rehearsal, listened for a while and wondered: what kind of pianist is this?

She thought she knew him from somewhere, but couldn't place him.

The last time she heard him he was 17 years old and podgy.

Four days later, in an unheated and dirty concert hall in Qingdao, with amplifying equipment that gave off a mezzo-forte buzz, there was an out-of-tune Baldwin grand piano, with a broken A flat above middle C. When you struck the key, a lot of other notes sounded, but not the A flat. The B rattled too.

The hastily summoned piano tuner didn't appear. Levit changed the programme: he didn't play Waldstein, but instead seven of the twelve Transcendental Études by Liszt, which he learned a long time ago but had never played in public. 'The most sacred passage in Waldstein is the bit in the minor key in the second movement with the diminished fifth, and for that I need the A flat', Igor explained to the flummoxed critic. 'That was impossible on this piano, I knew that. I didn't know what would happen with Liszt. It was an experiment.' The experiment was successful.

On the four evenings that follow, apart from Waldstein and
Liszt, Igor plays Beethoven's Piano Concerto No. 5 Opus 73
in E flat major and Schubert's Moments musicaux. He accompanied Beethoven violin sonatas and Lieder recitals. A bravura
performance.

On the bus journey from Jinan to Qingdao, Eleonore Büning
watched Levit practising the piano concerto: score on his
knees, keyboard in his head, an Alfred Brendel recording in
his ears.

'First of all I always learn a new piece from the score without a
piano. I carry it around with me in my head, and sometimes it
goes on for ages, months. You have to know it before you play
it. Then when I sit down and play it for the first time it isn't the
first time.' Levit said this not on the bus in China, but at home
on the phone when Eleonore Büning told him she wanted to
write a profile of him and had two more questions. He was in
the student canteen when she called.

A profile in the *Frankfurter Allgemeine* of a pianist who hadn't
even sat his concert exams, and hasn't made a CD apart from
a recording of the Diabelli Variations, is unusual.

'He wasn't even on the public radar', Büning would say on
WDR. 'But I was – and still am – so convinced of his artistic
integrity. I'm not talking about his technical skill, a lot of
people have that, and technically he's unimpeachable. But the
expressive power, the intensity, the creativity of this musician
– I'd never experienced anything like it in the whole of my
career.' She decided to tell the world.

The article was published on 3 May 2010, and didn't begin very
flatteringly.

'Six years ago I heard Igor Levit for the first time. He was 17, a round little person and incredibly chatty. He poked his nose in everywhere, told unfunny jokes, had something to say about every subject, and it was only when he was sitting at the piano and playing that this fat child temporarily stopped talking.'

But then.

'What distinguishes great pianists? That they flawlessly master the most difficult literature. But above all: that they know something about life, and how it is reflected and elevated through the development and structure, the history and message of the music: so that they can open up the pieces they play the way you open a book and read it, and that they tell us their stories as if they had just happened for the first time, so that we understand it all easily, with our ears and our hearts.'

The article is one of those ones that music critics only get to write a few times in their lives and only when they can't quite believe what they are hearing. 'With Levit, music comes into being in his head, not on the keys', Eleonore Büning wrote. 'In most rising young pianists, even the very gifted ones, it's exactly the other way around.'

She concluded with a sentence that would linger in Igor's mind for a long time to come.

'So the people of Bad Kissingen can retrospectively pat themselves on the back and say: a great year. But Igor Levit, unlike ... all the other nice compliant attractive, mechanical reelers-off of notes that the PR machine throws up from time to time, has what it takes to become one of the great pianists of the century. Or rather, he is already.'

Igor knew that the profile had been published, but not how important it would be. He saw the paper at a filling station near his parents' house, and asked the man at the till if he could take a look inside. Then he bought the whole stack.

The whole industry read the article. His future press agent Maren Borchers. And the man who gave him the contract with his record company. On that Sunday, in May 2010, a new chapter began.

#

When Maren Borchers finished reading Eleonore Büning's article, she called her up and shouted at her down the phone. How can you write a piece like that? she asked. How can you lay such a burden on somebody? How can you set the bar so high? He's still a baby, he can only lose.

Eleonore Büning replied that she knew all that – but you only get to write such a piece once in your life, and this was it.

Months later, in January 2011, Eleonore Büning had her Bechstein grand refurbished – and invited Igor to give a house concert in the sitting room of her flat in an old building in Berlin. It was her birthday, and she had invited Berlin artists, fellow arts journalists, important contacts, friends and Maren Borchers.

Borchers' husband came with her. She had to promise him not to spend all evening working as she usually did on such evenings.

When they turned up, Büning took Igor and Maren Borchers by the hands, led them into the music library and closed the door from outside, saying: you two need to talk.

Borchers knew Igor only from Büning's article, and had never heard him play. Igor knew her from an interview of which he remembered only the headline: 'I don't take on prodigies.'

They talked briefly, about this and that.

Then Igor had to play. Beethoven, the 'Tempest'. Eleonore Büning wept with happiness. After the concert Igor and Borchers arranged to meet for a coffee in the Literaturhaus. When they met she said: 'We don't have to work together. We can, if we want. But we don't have to.' Her words made an impression.

This was the day when Igor's collaboration with his press agent began. A woman who says that, without her, Igor wouldn't have become who he is today.

That's exactly how Igor sees things too.

'I haven't got that many human constants in my life', Igor says, 'and I'm not really after constants. But if they show up of their own accord, I'm not going to let go of them. Maren is a constant, and she will remain one. I'm not giving her up.'

Maren Borchers spent the first two years turning down requests for interviews. There wasn't yet anything worth advertising.

When she set up a Facebook page for her agency, she suggested to Igor: do a public rehearsal in the Maison de France. We'll invite people via Facebook and see what happens.

No one came.

The articles published about Igor were divided into two camps.

There were colleagues who disagreed with Eleonore Büning. And there were those who were enthusiastic about Igor, tried and tested critics as well as authors who didn't usually write about classical music.

After this Igor became increasingly noisy on Twitter, and the twin soundtracks ran in parallel.

Maren Borchers' operating principle: the artist should be able to concentrate on art. He needs a milieu that makes that possible for him – a milieu that he blindly trusts.

Except that Igor's intention wasn't to concentrate solely on his art.

#

It's not the result of a strategy that Igor is as visible a presence away from the concert hall as he is in it.

But neither is it completely unplanned.

Maren Borchers tried to get him to focus. Igor did a lot of what he did because Borchers had orchestrated it. He did a lot more because Borchers couldn't stop him. Igor's strategy was one of maximum concentration – except on lots of things at the same time.

'Things are the way they are today not least because of how we worked', Maren Borchers says. 'If we'd passed Igor around the talk shows like ripe fruit from the get-go, we wouldn't be where we are now.' Not any more.

Before founding her agency Borchers had worked for a classical music label and met a tenor who very quickly became successful. He asked her to advise him, told her she was the only person in the field that he trusted. She warned him: do less. Less. Even less. Don't go on that TV show, don't go on that one, don't go on the glitzy late-night chat show – leave that for now, just wait! But it wasn't going fast enough for him. She gave him advice, he ignored her warnings and eventually she said: Fine, you've decided to burn the candles at both ends. His career didn't last. She wasn't going to let that happen again.

It was imperative that Igor didn't spread himself too thinly. He was too much anyway.

Today she devotes most of her working time, energy and resources to Igor; he has her permission to call at any time, day or night, and he makes full use of it. 'Igor lives in my phone', she says. His ring tone in her phone is Goldberg Variation No. 14, played by Igor himself.

'I trust him completely', Maren Borchers says. 'And anyway, it's not entirely up to us. I would always count on the good in people. But if someone wants to provoke an argument with Igor, they'll do it anyway.

'I would have left long ago if I had the feeling the guy was a dick. It's exactly the opposite. And as soon as he stopped listening, our collaboration would be over anyway – there would be no point.'

Does it make life hard for her that he feels so politically ambitious? 'Not at all. On the contrary. He expands my horizon enormously.' And what about him? Does it make his life difficult? Wouldn't it be easier to do things differently?' She thinks for a moment. 'No.'

#

Hanover, 1 November 2019. A cold, dark day, the hall in the University of Music is sold out. Igor is giving his inaugural concert as a professor at the same university where he spent over ten years as a student. Igor's family are there, his teachers, old friends. Before the break he plays the Adagio from Symphony No. 10 by Gustav Mahler, in a version by the Scottish composer and pianist Ronald Stevenson. After the break comes Stevenson's Passacaglia on DSCH, the initials of Dmitri Shostakovich translated into notes. A piece that hardly anyone knows and hardly any other pianist can play, a circumnavigation of the world in sounds, a history of humanity, a journey through a life, 90 minutes long.

Two works that are much too big for the piano.

'The Passacaglia is a political, left-wing, international piece. Sensationally well written. Incredibly deep, serious, expansive, sprawling, very emotional. And it touches me; there's a lot I can do with it. It all fits with the way I play. The manic, the political, dark, hard, sensual, it's all very close to me.'

If he had been able to play the Passacaglia in 2014, he would have recorded it at the time, along with the Goldberg and Diabelli Variations, and 'The People United Will Never Be Defeated!', Igor says. 'I see those four works as the most important cycles of variations in the literature. But at the time I just couldn't play the Passacaglia. I like having time on stage. I like pieces that give me time.'

But pieces that give more time than others are also more expensive to perform.

'We'd never experienced a concert like that before', his mother says. 'Not because of the length of the piece but because of the intensity and density of the information that he sends into the audience. We were completely exhausted afterwards. And it wasn't boring for a moment. I was worried, I thought: my God, who's come along to this? Who's sitting in the hall? What are their expectations? I didn't say that to Igor, but those were my thoughts. He needs those extreme situations, he seeks them too. And then I realise the 90 minutes are up, and I'd like to go on hearing the story.'

\#

On a train journey from Hanover to Berlin our conversation returns to the Passacaglia.

– What happens to you during those one and a half hours? Do you notice what's happening in the auditorium? Or are you completely immersed in the music?

– I see everything, I'm aware of everything, I'm focused on myself and on everyone else at the same time. I pick up the atmosphere, the mood of the people in the hall. And when I notice that I'm losing my attention, I grab it back again. I heighten the intensity. I play with the tempo, the timing. I'm quite good at that. I never impose a plan; I always take my bearings from how the space works. Then I give it a bit more juice – or else I burrow my way even further into the piano. Or else I hesitate; I think to myself: no, I won't start yet, even though everyone's waiting for me. And perhaps today I fancy a different tempo.

– To what extent do you plan your playing in advance? How far can you look into the future within the works?

– Very far. But I have no problem deciding half a second before a particular moment: no, today, I'm going to take a different turning from the usual one. If I like it, I'll stay on the new path and if I don't, I'll just turn off again. Then I give it twenty horsepower less, or more. I'm actually both: far ahead, but also right in the moment. I know what's coming, and I'm free to decide again at any point.

– But that means you're thinking about the piece while you're playing?

– I hardly ever think: I've got to play this passage in such and such a way, to be honest. I'm mentally inside the piece, but I'm almost always thinking about people.

– How often do you need to have played a piece until it all works like that?

– I don't think you can prepare yourself so well that that it's all there at the first performance. There are pieces I play for the first time, and I know they're not yet fully developed. The last 15 per cent only comes with playing. And I wouldn't be keen on playing them at home until I was 100 per cent there. Eventually the point has come where I have to take it on stage so that it can go on developing.

– How do you practise?

– All the time, in my head. Manually I find a lot of things – touch wood – not that difficult, once I've been through them in my head; it makes a lot of things superfluous. It's hard to describe in the abstract what happens there. I'm thinking of a particular moment from a particular piece. It has a particular sound inside me. Then I work on that sound – until the passage sounds the way I want it to in my head. And then I try to translate that idea into reality on the piano. I think to myself: how do I get a particular vibration, a particular timing, a particular tempo so that this passage sounds the way it does in my head?

– But does that mean that in the concert every note sounds the way it's supposed to?

– No, that wouldn't work at all. Because in my imagination I have no barriers. I can imagine that a particular passage sounds like it's in a cathedral, whispered, shouted or sounding like it's in a toilet. Then I try and translate that sound as well as I can – but it's only ever an approach, striving for an idea. Of course a piano always sounds like a piano. That's why I can't work out a new piece from the piano. It doesn't work. If I'm only working at the piano, my imagination is limited.

– How tough is all that?

– I find letting go after concerts tougher. That's why sometimes after the Beethoven Sonata Opus 111 I tell jokes. Not because I find them funny at that moment, but to free myself from the music as quickly as possible. I have to get rid of that mood, quickly and brutally; I don't want to stay in it. And I force all the people around me out as well. That's also why I hate talking about the concert after it's finished. Sometimes that's difficult for other people, I know, but I don't want to. Then I always feel that I need to take myself more seriously than I really am.

Maybe that's also the secret to why Igor sounds the way he sounds: because he doesn't engage further with the piano in his imagination.

It would be interesting to hear what it sounds like inside his head.

#

Hamburg, 18 November 2019, a chilly autumn Sunday evening. Igor is on the stage of the Elbphilharmonie. It's the third evening of his Hamburg Beethoven cycle, and tonight the programme includes the Sonata Opus 57 in F minor, known as the Appassionata.

But today's a bit different from usual, as you can tell from the moment he walks on stage. He's tense. There's none of the lightness, the mastery, the nonchalance of that first evening. He plays with fire in his belly and, he tells me later, in the face of a coming cold. But that's not all.

He's struggling.

Today the music doesn't sound triumphant and invincible as it did before, but quite different: Igor sounds vulnerable, still far from shaky. But when listening it becomes clear that he could break down at any moment and the music would collapse in on itself.

If you were inclined to be dramatic, you might say: on the first evening, with the Waldstein Sonata, Igor was the creator of a universe according to Beethoven's blueprint; at every moment he was controlled and masterful. That energy is missing today. Instead, the notes also convey a certainty that Igor doesn't just have to produce them, but also tame them and hold them together. And today that's costing him a lot more effort than it has on other evenings. There's no miracle happening; it's clearer than usual today that this is just a human being playing.

'I don't remember that evening, but yes, probably there was some kind of tension. There was a lot going on at the time. I was getting a lot of messages, most of them hostile. It was constant. Those were the first waves. I knew the AfD [the far-right Alternative für Deutschland party] were starting to call me out. It was very much in the air. Basically it was just a matter of time before more things happened.'

In the Elbphilharmonie the rows of seats are organized around the stage, most of them in such a way that the audience aren't looking up at the stage but down on it. And while you see him working away down there on the grand piano, it makes his achievement look all the greater. A naïve thought: what madness it is, what lunacy that a human being is even capable of playing these pieces.

\#

Three days before the concert Igor was sitting in ZDF's Berlin studio. He had wanted to be a guest on a political talk show, and this one is a panel that he's been invited onto not only as a classical music star, but primarily to discuss his views as a politically thinking person. Now, on presenter Maybrit Illner's popular show, he's going to talk about 'hatred on the web'. A subject that you really can't, in a television debate, be in two minds about. But the other panellists are prominent figures: apart from Igor, the Green politician Cem Özdemir; Dorothee Bär, State Minister for Digital Infrastructure; the internet activist Sascha Lobo; and Ralf Schuler, director of the parliamentary desk of the tabloid *BILD-Zeitung*. In him, the producers had found someone who didn't exactly advocate hatred on the web, but who was willing to argue in controversial terms. He's the only member of the panel who thinks it's a second-order problem.

Maybrit Illner: 'Igor Levit, when we're actually fighting hate speech – so, violence in language – are we fighting the cause, or does hate speech have another cause?

Igor: 'In my opinion language is what sets the tone. I mean, I have no language in what I do. I go about the place

non-verbally, I make music, I produce states. I can't explain
them, but once again, what you can't explain in language sets
the tone. And sitting here and saying: sure, you can hurl hatred
and provocation at somebody, or you can say, "I'll execute you,"
that's not so bad, because I'm not going to do it – that's really
not an argument. That's the seed from which these actions
emerge. And I really think it's dangerous to make that seem
less important than it is.'

The audience applauds. While the applause is still going on
Ralf Schuler begins a prepared manoeuvre against Igor, and
quotes a four-year-old tweet.

'But my dear Mr Levit', Schuler says, 'you yourself have
said on Twitter that the AfD is made up of people who
have forfeited their own humanity. When you were inter-
viewed by *Der Spiegel* you said you don't regret a word. By
saying that you exclude yourself from any kind of humane
discourse. If you dispute the humanity of human beings,
you're out.'

Igor posted the tweet that Schuler is referring to on 1
November 2015. The previous evening the national TV
magazine programme *Panorama* broadcast a piece in which
an AfD MP from Bremen claimed in passing that a refugee in
his constituency had raped a 12-year-old girl. 'If something like
that happens and you don't intervene for reasons of political
correctness and arrest the perpetrator, you have anarchy.'
When questioned on the subject, the MP explained that he
didn't know exactly where and when the rape had happened,
and when he was questioned further the matter proved to be
unfounded. Igor, who came across the video of the broadcast
on Twitter, was furious. He shared the tweet, added a coarse
insult to it, linked to the AfD's Twitter feed and commented:
'people who have forfeited their humanity'.

The tweet caused waves. 'That message was scandalous: to deny humanity to one's political opponent, however distasteful they may be, indicates not a tolerant philosophy, but a totalitarian one', *Die Welt* commented. Levit should learn not immediately to tweet the first thing that comes into his head. Other publications took a similar view. The tenor as whole was Levit is going too far.

But Igor felt he had been misunderstood. 'Mr Schuler, as a child I learned that the word "Mensch" is a Yiddish word. A Mensch is a good human being. A Mensch is an honourable human being. Now let's talk about the case in point. An MP from Bremen or somewhere around there looked into the camera in a national TV studio and said: we've got anarchy here right now. In my district, my constituency, a girl has just been raped by a refugee. That's where the axe goes in. That was in 2015, the mood was already quite dangerous, and then it took a question from the journalist. Where did it happen? And who was it? The house of cards collapsed, and the guy could only stammer and say yes, you've got me. Please excuse me. On the basis of the fact that a Mensch, a human being, is an honourable one. Has this human being forfeited that honour for me? And I stand by that. There's nothing I would take back. That's dangerous.' Ralf Schuler, without looking Igor in the eye, replies: 'If Article 1 of the Constitution ['The dignity of the human person is inviolable and inalienable'] doesn't apply as far as you're concerned, I'll take that on board. But strictly speaking I ought to get up and leave.'

Minutes later this dialogue was up on YouTube and going around the right-wing networks; Igor's tweet from 2015 was dredged up as well.

Three days later, on the evening of his Hamburg concert, Igor's management receives a death threat. An hour before the concert is due to start, an email comes in: soon the audience will have the shock of their lives, and after that Igor, the 'Jewish pig', won't need any more concert dates; he'll be silenced right in front of an audience. It was put pretty much like that; only Igor and the police know the exact wording. On the evening that the threat refers to, Igor was playing Brahms in Wiesbaden with the Deutsche Kammerphilharmonie Bremen.

At first Maren Borchers and Kristin Schuster decided not to say anything to Igor so as not to endanger the concert. They started researching what needs to be done, and informed the local criminal investigation office.

'I got back the next day. I didn't know anything about it, that day I didn't know anything. The next day I travelled back. Maren gave me a call and said, I'll pick you up from the station, there's a thing I need to do there. I didn't know what she was talking about. Maren has to do something at the station? And then she collected me from the platform, and at that moment I knew and said: There are death threats?'

When he found out what was going on, the first thing he wanted to do was to read the email. He wanted to confront the sender; ideally, he wanted to go and stand outside his front door with a camera crew. But identifying the sender was much harder than they imagined, as the mail came from the dark web, and even investigators had trouble discovering its source.

The police imposed a strict information embargo, and anyone who wasn't supposed to know anything was kept in the dark. Not even Igor's parents were informed. No organizers pulled out, the tour with the Deutsche Kammerphilharmonie Bremen went ahead as planned, and the performance mentioned in the threat passed without incident.

It wasn't until just before New Year that Igor went public. 'I'm worried', he wrote in his essay in the newspaper *Der Tagesspiegel*, 'but not for me. I'm worried for our country.'

A week after the Hamburg concert in November the Lucerne Festival posts a short video, just a minute long – in Lucerne Igor is performing the Beethoven cycle in parallel with Hamburg. It's an edit of the last few bars of the Appassionata. Igor, with a radically short haircut, in a loosely fitting white shirt, teeth clenched, hammers the finale into the keys. Only a few days have passed since his performance in Hamburg, but he is barely recognizable. The rage is no longer hidden in the music, it has come into the open. And his playing has achieved a new quality. For a long time it really seemed as if he didn't need to defend his music with words. The finale of the Appassionata defended his words through the medium of music.

\#

Igor has often talked about the first time he was openly confronted with anti-Semitism.

'I was at a dinner in Hessen. An affluent, very comfortable group, at first glance everything very pleasant and nice. I'd given a private concert before the dinner, this was in 2011, so I must have been 24. It was the phase just after my exam, when I didn't yet have a record company, or anyone else who wanted to work with me.

I was sitting next to a lawyer in his early to mid-forties, and we chatted, and he asked how things were going.

I said: not bad, I'm playing this and that, I told him about the exam, about the article in the *Frankfurter Allgemeine Zeitung*. I also talked about my search for a record company; that was a big topic for me. The lawyer listened to it all – and suddenly he turns the conversation around and says: well, you're obviously hard to market. I asked why I should be hard to market? And he started talking about culture, about belonging and being foreign. It was a completely bizarre situation, and all of a sudden he said: You've grown up with your parents in Germany, and I think that's great. But you must never forget that you belong to an ethnic group that might live here, but wasn't expected to live here any more.

I had no idea what he was talking about. At that moment I just thought he was a bit rude.

I only understood a few months later – when I was talking to Maxim about it, Maxim Biller. I met him in the Adlon in Berlin, at a party for the tenth birthday of the *Frankfurter Allgemeine Sonntagzeitung.* He was standing in the smoking room. I didn't smoke, but I thought the more interesting people would probably be in there, and we chatted – he was the first person I felt was really listening to me. He said, Igor, that wound never heals. And he was right.

The words had been an attempt at an erasure. The theoretical erasure of my existence. This man was saying to me: you don't exist. You have no right to be. And that lack of a right to be is the essential psychological sore point in my life.

Maxim soon put me in touch with the journalist Georg Diez. They did a lot to help me understand it all and to see connections. I learned a huge amount during that time, not just nice things. They explained to me what anti-Semitism really is, what racism is, how systematized hatred works, what contempt for humanity can do and what's already been done with it. With me too, even though I mightn't have properly understood it before.

In the end that evening in Hessen led to a great feeling of alienation, a feeling of 'you lot' and 'me'.

There are lots of similar situations. After a concert at the Berlin Philharmonie, when I was signing CDs, I was congratulated by a couple saying the Bach had been astonishing, given that I lacked the cultural bond for the piece. An ARD reporter said it must be special for me to play in Israel, after all it's my home. That was six months ago. He told me he had a lot of Jewish friends who were going to Israel now because they felt safer there. I asked him: are you telling me I'm in danger here, do you want me to go? Later I got the weird apology that he hadn't been aware of the significance of the topic. What significance? There is no significance. I'm at home here, this is my home. End of story.

There's also the perfidious variation: goodness, Mr Levit, you put so much energy into opposing anti-Semitism – how does that sit with the fact that you like telling Jewish jokes in public? Things like that happen. Sometimes subtly, sometimes less subtly. I choke when I hear things like that. Then you've got someone applying the eraser and simply rubbing me out.

I want to be allowed to exist. In my previous life there were lots of things that I wanted to be and couldn't. I fought for lots of things, everything in fact, even when I was a boy. And now all of a sudden in the eyes of this one man, that time in Hessen, I couldn't exist at all. There were many such moments, and I know how to deal with them now – because I can categorize them.

Since I've been giving piano recitals, I've been everything: the German pianist, the Russian pianist, the Russian-German, German-Russian, German with Jewish roots, Russian with

Jewish roots, Russian-German with Jewish roots. It was relatively rare that I was 'the pianist'.

But the only side of me that was never in question as far as I was concerned was the pianist. It was always there, even if I had to assert myself with it outwardly. Everything else was constantly in question: the activist, the teacher, this, that, the other. Everything disputed and fought for, with sport, with literature, with a huge amount of work, I constantly have to deliver proof that I'm capable of doing what I want to do. I've even held on to a lot of friendships – by making an effort for them and going on doing so.

And even if it might sound like this: those words back in Hessen were no help to me. Not in the slightest. But understanding the insult as an insult – that helped me see things more clearly.

The last ten years have been one long hardening process for me. My language became quicker and more concise, I became clearer. Not towards the people I love. But with the outside world. I try to keep my door open at all times; I don't wear armour. There aren't many people I've opened the door for, but one thing is clear: if I'm in the middle of a television programme, in 2019, and a journalist from the Springer tabloid press ensures with a single sentence that the life of a Jew in Germany is in danger, and I'm very clear what I'm saying with these words: Then the door is closed.'

Some people are troubled by Igor not least because he stops them from forgetting that anti-Semitism still exists.

#

Igor doesn't understand how it can be: how people willingly and unprotestingly follow him through complex musical works, but can't follow a clear and simple logic according to which one human being should not treat another human being worse than he would wish to be treated himself.

Most other pianists – pretty much all of them, in fact – sell themselves through their inoffensiveness. Above all of this is the desire that is much more than a wish, it's a premiss: don't annoy anybody. Don't do anything that could bother anybody, so: don't publicly criticize, best of all don't adopt a position. In the eyes of those that don't share a position, it looks wrong. It's a fear-driven way of thinking, impelled by concern about making mistakes.

Igor doesn't have that fear, and for him there is no boundary between music and the thought that goes beyond it. In his view, art, music, is unthinkable without the adoption of a position; every individual bar, every single note is a statement of belief. So why should he be any different here.

What he has to say is not complex. Many journalists have accused him of triviality for that reason, as if the truth needs to be complicated. What he has to say is very simple. And the clarity with which he expresses simple things is captivating – because he doesn't act as if it were anything but a very simple truth, and as if there were no point in him actually coming out with it.

He says: do the right thing, open your eyes, don't stop listening, pay attention to other people. Obvious things. He says: don't do shitty stuff. He signals: look, easy as that.

Igor really arrives through the effect he causes. Through the non-verbal. Like all pianists, but he's one of the few to do it away from the piano as well.
His stylistic device: determination.

At the moment when he speaks – as someone who mightn't per se be expected to do so – he also points towards the significance of speech.

His message: who says you have to turn away from reality in order to turn towards art?

For Igor, music isn't inoffensive, it isn't neutral ground; he forces his audience into a position: acceptance or rejection. Neutral listening is barely possible.

#

To the people who accuse him of putting himself at the centre of things too much, of saying 'I' too often, he has this to say:

'We live in a country that doesn't like people who say "I" for various reasons, some of them historical. My honest answer: the accusation bores me. Let them argue with me, let them find an idea or a project ridiculous. Then they should develop their own idea. In that case I'll be happy for them and I'll support them in it. I'm completely serious about that. But that criticism bores me. What am I supposed to say but "I"? What else is a person supposed to say? I'm certainly not going to stop doing it just because someone criticizes me for it.'

It takes a while to work out that there's nothing self-important about his 'I'. There's no egomania in it, no claim to universal validity; he doesn't mean it in a big way, but in a small and subjective one. It's an 'only I'.

#

Igor's sense of himself as a politically thinking person begins with his friendship with Georg Diez – the journalist, author and *Spiegel* columnist for many years. He's a friend and confidant to Igor, and also a teacher and a source of inspiration. They met in 2011 via Maxim Biller.

'"Schorsch" is much older than me and infinitely better read. He can put things into words that I couldn't put into words before. I learned it from him. He developed my thinking, changed it and made it more grown-up. He gave me books to read. I saw what he read and read what he wrote, and I started thinking.'

The journey begins in 2008. Igor is on a cruise ship, where he's been employed as a concert pianist, and he's reading about the collapse of the Lehman Brothers investment bank.

A little later the Greek crisis begins. Igor is shaken by the icy cold with which German politicians talk about the country and its population – and the cynicism with which *BILD-Zeitung* sneers at the supposedly lazy Greeks.

'At that moment it became clear to me how the right way of thinking works – all of a sudden there were forces that defined a "we" and a "you lot", who said: the others are taking something away from us.'

Igor talks regularly about the situation with a woman friend who comes from Greece, and she tells him about the mood in the country. For Igor, the Greek crisis becomes a moment of awakening – the first.

The second moment of awakening comes in 2015, when thousands of people from Syria and other countries flee across the Mediterranean to Europe.

'For the first time in my life I saw life at the other end of the world – people who were suddenly standing here and saying:

I'm here, I'm a human being, I'm standing here, I want to live, please help me. And I also saw that the right in this country, after a brief moment of clarity, decided to say: No, you're only a third-class person. I urgently wanted to differentiate myself from this new icy German coldness.'

Igor started to express himself on Twitter. He quickly learned how the platform worked and how he could effectively find an audience there.

And he also knew that Twitter on its own wouldn't achieve anything. He began to engage, to help people in a concrete sense as well, with money and contacts.

Some people whom Igor had previously seen as friends distanced themselves from him – as he did from them, seeing them now as anti-Semites and racists.

He started reading other books, other stories, other narratives, works by American authors, particularly James Baldwin, whom he idolizes.

'I'm a European, and a very committed one. I won't let these people talk down this Europe, this cooperation, this society, by playing with anxieties. In my little world in which I live and in which I can raise my voice, I will argue against those people who treat this community like a piece of paper that you screw up and throw away. I'm a citizen of the world first and foremost. That implies a certain responsibility. I'm a very political person. I always have been, and am more and more so.'

#

In the spring of 2016, Igor and Georg Diez travel to Greece, to the refugee camp in Idomeni on the border with Macedonia, where thousands of people who have fled across the Mediterranean to Greece are holding out. On the day of their arrival, the press report that the camp has been cleared.

'We met two young men walking past us along the railway lines. Georg asked them: Where have you come from? From Libya, they say. And where do you want to get to? Idomeni. There's no Idomeni left, we said. They looked at each other and then simply slumped onto the gravel on the track bed. For the first time I saw people who had lost the most essential thing in their lives: their direction. They could walk to the left or to the right; it made no difference. All of a sudden they were in the void; they didn't know where to go. That was a very dark moment.'

A young man, educated and eloquent, speaks very good English, taught French literature and history at Aleppo University, now stands in the middle of a refugee camp, holding a shard of mirror and trying to shave. Igor championed his cause, managed to help him, and years later the pair are still in contact.

'That might be one of the reasons why I think about freedom so much. I've come to understand how valuable it is to be able to say: I'm free to move about. I'm free to formulate my goals.

'What I've seen are the consequences of political decisions – many of them made by politicians in Germany who lay claim to their humanity. They are decisions which mean that hundreds of thousands of people are suddenly stripped of their direction. That recognition started a lot of logs rolling for me – and politically it took me to a new level.'

#

Igor's political modus operandi is reaction. He doesn't pursue an agenda of his own; he himself seldom raises subjects, but he doesn't avoid them either. About where he locates himself politically – beyond concrete issues – we know only the phrase that he uses repeatedly in interviews: 'I'm extra-extra-extra left'. But what does that mean?

In public Igor soon came to be known as the pianist who delivered speeches before the concert. For Igor – unlike for many of his listeners – this wasn't a breaking of the fourth wall but a completely organic extension. He was up on stage anyway, sharing himself with the audience, so why not say a few words too? The idea: in the concert hall people listen to one another, it may be the core of their shared humanity.

'I know I'm forcing something on the audience at that moment. It's absolutely a liminal experience: going on stage, taking a piece of paper out of your pocket and speaking unannounced for between two and ten minutes. That unsettles the audience, rightly, and it isn't easy for me either. It's much easier to talk at a Green Party rally, where the people expect you to say something, unlike on a concert stage. I'm absolutely open to people saying: this isn't all right, I don't want to hear it. I do it anyway, but I think it's ok if somebody says I don't want this.'

#

The day after the night when Donald Trump wins the US Presidential election, Igor is supposed to be playing a recital of Beethoven sonatas in the Palais des Beaux-Arts in Brussels, including the Appassionata. He played the same programme two days before in the Wigmore Hall in London.

On the night before the Brussels concert, he didn't get a minute's sleep. He was beside himself, not with fury, but with helplessness that turned now and then into despair.

Everything was coming together.

First the concert in London, the capital of the country that had decided to leave the European Union six months previously.

Then the concert in the capital of the European Union, which had been thrown into the biggest crisis since its foundation by the announcement of Brexit.

A sleepless night.

And Trump.

These were days when it felt as if the ground was shaking. Because a few very fundamental certainties that were previously as reliable as the laws of nature no longer seemed to apply. Top and bottom, left and right, good and evil, right and wrong. These were days when many people were starting to feel as if it wasn't enough to think you were silently on the right side, since more and more people, not all of them silent, were switching to the other side. Igor, sleepless and in turmoil, decided to say a few words before the concert in the evening. Not to put anyone back on the right path. And not – as he is accused of doing even today – postulating a political programme. He spoke because the things he says weighed heavily on his mind.

'Please allow me to say a few words before I start.'

He wrote the speech on the Eurostar to Brussels, sentence for sentence, as if intoxicated. By the end it was a whole page. Much too much, in fact, almost six minutes in all.

He talked about how his parents, his sister and he came to Germany in 1995. How they came to give him and his sister the best start in life, so that they could become whatever they wanted to be. And so that they didn't just become intelligent people, but citizens who were aware of their responsibility for their country, their friends, the people around them.

'Since then, every time I'm asked whether I consider myself as a Russian or a German, my answer has been clear: I'm a European. Not a proud one, but a grateful, respectful, politically thinking, curious and responsible European who is a musician by profession.

'But today is a dark day, and behind us lies a dark night. Yesterday the greatest economic power in the world elected a bigoted opportunist, a furious, dangerous man as their President. For over a year the US election has left us shattered, along with our understanding of decency and respect. Yesterday's election put this man in the most important office in the world.

'Fear, alienation, aggression, darkness and negativity have led over 50 million people to vote for him. But that isn't the first time that such a tragedy has happened.'

Igor, standing on the stage of the Palais des Beaux-Arts, looked into many friendly, appreciative faces. The audience wasn't expecting this, he could tell.

'We have experienced millions of people in the United Kingdom deciding to leave the EU, on the basis of false assertions and fear. We see a presidential candidate in France throwing the country into fear and terror. In my homeland, Germany, I see neo-fascists sowing fear and mistrust, undermining the bonds that keep us together. We are seeing this development in many different countries.

'And what are we doing? How is my generation responding? So far we've allowed their words to destroy our societies. Politicians speak about the European Union as if it's rubbish. The European Union is a creation of peace and unity. Does the EU make mistakes? Of course. Does the EU sometimes leave me disappointed and furious? And how. But it's my EU. I'm a part of it, we all are. The EU has transformed our part of the world, which was for so long a theatre of war and conflict, into a peaceful place; it has brought us all together with the same goals. And we allow these people to spit on it? How dare they?

'Since last night one thing has been clear to me. The time of remaining in my comfort zone is over for me. As long as I have a voice and as long as I can raise it, I will not allow these people to destroy our society, our world. We can't allow that to happen. We must do what we can to ...'

A voice from the auditorium tells Igor to shut his mouth and play.

'... keep our society human and intact.'

This was only to be expected; for purely statistical reasons in every audience of this size there must be a certain number of anti-Europeans, nationalists, non-sympathizers. Even so he flinches for a moment, but doesn't let it show.

'Get out of here', someone else shouts, this time meaning not Igor, but the person who was shouting before.

'No', Igor replies. 'Don't throw him out. You stay here.'

Then he goes on, by now clearly speaking for longer than five minutes.

'I know life isn't a concert hall. But music is life, it's all of us being here together. You listen to me, I listen to you. Listening to one another – that's civilization. The great music that we share creates a bond between us and reminds us of the best thing that human life can create and share. We shouldn't wait any longer. We're citizens of our countries, we belong to Europe, we have friendly connections with the United States. We can raise our voice and we should raise our voice. Let us stay strong, stay together, let us fight for humanity, for trust, for mutual respect and for belief in other people. And let us not only do it while we sit in this beautiful concert hall, but every day, at every hour that we can.'

Some of these words would be a touch too grandiose and too dramatic outside of a concert hall, but none of these sentences was so new or controversial that almost everyone in the hall would not agree with them. But as we have said: this wasn't a sermon or a lecture. He wasn't going to persuade anyone here today, he was quite clear about that. Igor said all of this because he needed the feeling of being among like-minded people.

'And now to Beethoven.'

From that moment onwards, Igor was the pianist for whom being a pianist wasn't enough.

Shortly before he stepped onto the stage in Brussels, he posted the text of his speech on Twitter. More than 400 people shared it, and a huge number of people continue to post congratulations and agreement, even years later. One of them also wrote 'revolting polemic by a typical quota Jew', but was almost drowned out by the mass of agreement.

But that doesn't mean that Igor doesn't clearly remember that one person even years later.

#

His contact with Die Grünen, the Green Party, was made via Maren Borchers, who is a friend of the MP Konstantin von Notz. He gave Igor a guided tour of the Reichstag and introduced him to Green Party MPs Claudia Roth, Katrin Göring-Eckardt, Cem Özdemir and Robert Habeck.

'The prevailing mood in the party is one of seriousness, of great empathy – and a fundamental understanding of the changing times that we find ourselves in', Igor says. 'I think that's essential for a party. Of course there are also issues where I disagree.'

But much more than the content, first and foremost it's the people that Igor is interested in.

'We just got on very well. I had been close to the party for a long time without being a member – that was how contact was established and maintained. Real friendships came about.'

Before the 2018 European election rally in Leipzig, Habeck asked Igor whether he could imagine playing piano for the delegates.

'It was a very relaxed, very easy and every natural story. In that time leading up to the European elections, I had the feeling: this party is almost the only one that isn't trying to overtake the others on the right.'

Igor came on and said a few words, then played the transcription of the Ode to Joy from Beethoven's Symphony No. 9, the European anthem. And the Aria from the Goldberg Variations.

One of his sentences particularly stands out: 'I'm just a citizen. I learned in year five or six at school that democracy without citizens' responsibility doesn't work. It's as uncomplicated as that.'

In the summer of 2019, long after the party rally, Igor spent a few days in the mountains with a friend.

'We were sitting there and I said: just wait, I think in six months' time I'll get my first death threats, and I'd rather not be alone when that happens. I'd rather be part of a community in which I know I have a secure roof over my head.'

During the time of the death threats, Claudia Roth, Konstantin von Notz and Cem Özdemir stood behind Igor like a family.

'To hell with artistic pseudo-neutrality. What is that even supposed to be? I feel close to these people, I've stepped inside their house. I think most of their political decisions are right, some not – but as regards the fundamentals, I haven't regretted my decision for a second.'

#

When Igor went public with the death threat, the reaction in the press was highly emotional. Little happened in the intervening years, and nothing of similar importance.

The spin was always the same: Igor, the musician who gets death threats.

But Igor sensed that the threat was not intended for him as a musician; he saw himself as being under attack not as a musician, but as a person.

'Anyone can become a target – the moment these fascists decide they don't like what you're doing. Regardless of whether you're an artist, a doctor, a politician or whoever. It is usually women and members of minorities. Often they fall silent and retreat.'

Igor was surprised by the surprise that the matter provoked. In an interview with the broadcaster Deutsche Welle he said he was startled to see that society as a whole didn't understand the urgency of the situation.

'These people feel empowered. They have political parties with members in parliament, who quite openly put forward an uncompromising neo-fascist political idea.'

He was troubled by the fact that issuing a death threat to a member of society is allowed – since it is not permitted, and hardly possible in any case, to track down the owner of the anonymous e-mail account. He was surprised that all of this could happen without any responsibility, because the perpetrators could not be pursued and traced.

The tone in which the matter was discussed in public made him furious.

'After every racist attack, after every assault, there's at least one politician who says: "Just to be clear, there is no room for racism in our country." But there's plenty of room for racism, unfortunately there's always been room for it. Get that into your heads! Stop throwing up smokescreens, stop talking as if we were five years old! Say it out loud: we have a very serious problem with racism and anti-Semitism. We should be a bit more grown-up with our language.'

#

Igor deliberately made the decision to show his face on Twitter.

He met up with Christopher Lauer, a digital strategist who once sat as a politician for the Pirate Party in the Berlin parliament. Lauer had a five-star number of Twitter followers, which impressed Igor. On a train journey from Frankfurt to Berlin he asked him to explain what Twitter was all about.

'Twitter was a liberation for me. I see it as a place of discovery, of thinking and writing. I can meet people there that I would probably never have met otherwise. I can read texts that I wouldn't have come across, follow conflicts that I previously had no idea about, and discover music, art and culture that's emerging right now at the other end of the world. I don't know who I would be today if I hadn't found all that.

Twitter for me means people, not institutions. A chorus of very different voices. A discursive orchestra.

And when I say liberation, I mostly mean emancipation. Twitter allows me to tell my story – and not only me, but literally everybody in the world. Independent of the logic and grammar of conventional media, quite direct and raw, tentative, furious, emphatic, searching, lost, happy – and always unfiltered and immediate. Twitter is an instrument that you need to learn and that you can master.

That can also be dangerous, without question. Above all, however, Twitter is intoxicating because it allows us to question power relations in a constructive way. Who am I, who are you? Who has control over the interpretation of my story?'

#

On New Year's Eve 2020, Igor drew up a plan.

'From now on I'm going to keep a few months of the year free. I'd like to spend time with the people who are important to me.

I keep absolutely no distance from music. But I do keep a proper distance from my profession. I ask myself more and more often: who am I really in this game? What is the justification for my existence as a musician?

It probably also had something to do with finishing the Beethoven sonatas. After the recording I wondered: I've spent half my life playing these pieces – and what do I do now?

At any rate it isn't enough for me just to manage my career. I'm not interested in that. I have a great fear of stagnation, a real, genuine fear. So what happens now?'

After conquering the mighty peaks of the piano literature, he was in search of the next project. He had spent his whole life with Beethoven, and didn't feel mature enough for Chopin.

He planned piano recital programmes for the next three years: first Beethoven, followed by the Stevenson Passacaglia.

And then?

'Rather than being pleased that I've got the Stevenson for the next three years, I'm worrying about what comes next. Basically I'm done with the Stevenson already. But what comes after it? It's a real problem. There are still two or three things that interest me. After that everything is open. I will always play the repertoire that I love. But during the year I need a hook that I can hold on to.'

Once again, the piano isn't enough for him. The repertoire that is genuinely considered as the piano repertoire isn't enough for him either. That's what draws him to pieces with a bit of megalomania about them.

'I'm interested in music that's bigger than the piano. And every Beethoven sonata, however small, is bigger. And it's all music that isn't just about music.'

These criteria sound banal, but they were far from easy to fulfil: the piece had to deal with subjects that mattered to him. It had to challenge and grip him – he had to want to play it.

Where was that going to lead?

One tentative answer to that is Sorabji. Kaikhosru Shapurji Sorabji, an almost contemporary composer, almost entirely unknown, even in the world of specialists. His works are music for musicians. Self-referential works that revolve around themselves, that don't speak of life, but of music. They're long, and difficult.

Was it worth it? Two years' work, for that?

'Of course I could learn it. Oh, I don't know.'

#

Berlin, 29 January 2020, a grey Wednesday morning. At about half past eight Igor arrives at the Paul Löbe Haus beside the Reichstag building. He's an hour early. But he wants to have a look at the exhibition before he plays at the opening later.

It's the memorial day for the victims of National Socialism, and the German Bundestag is showing works by the painter David

Olère in the foyer of the Paul Löbe Haus. They aren't pretty pictures; they show what many of the people being remembered today had to go through: everyday life in Auschwitz concentration camp. David Olère, born in Warsaw, lived in Berlin in the 1920s and worked as a sculptor and set painter. In 1943 he was arrested by the Gestapo in Paris, and deported to Auschwitz. There he belonged to a special unit that burned the corpses of its fellow inmates and shovelled the ashes out of the crematoria. He survived because he spoke English and secretly helped the SS to understand enemy radio news reports on the development of the war. Immediately after the liberation of the camp, he began to draw what he had seen: emaciated bodies, half-dead children, people abusing people. Doomed eyes, and the grimacing faces of the Nazis. At first Olère only made sketches, but soon he moved on to large-format oil paintings. They are the only pictorial sources of what happened in a concentration camp before the liberation. There are no words for the horror that they show.

Igor meanders alone through the still-deserted foyer, walks through the exhibition, looks in silence at the paintings. He had expected that they wouldn't leave him cold. He had not foreseen that they would disturb him to such an extent. But the idea of not looking, out of caution and self-protection, is out of the question. Everyone has to look, so he does too. But he doesn't just look, he feels the full emotional impact. And he feels attacked. He will still be talking about the paintings days later, but for now he takes his phone out of his jacket pocket and tweets.

'I was about to write what indescribable gratitude I feel to be able to play music here in the context of the David Olère exhibition opening. But having seen the paintings, one after the other, I feel an inner collapse like never before. There is no end to remembering. There must be no end to remembering.

There must never be a flight from pain and responsibility. And the fight against dehumanization, against fascism, against racism and against hatred must never end. Never. I have no more words.'

Soon there would be no eyewitnesses to the crimes of the past, either perpetrators or victims, Bundestag President Wolfgang Schäuble said at the opening. 'But the truth remains, and it remains a challenge. A challenge that each generation must face anew.' Igor, in a suit and with a black tie, sits down at the grand piano, takes off his glasses and plays first the chorale prelude 'Nun komm der Heiden Heiland', then the aria from the Goldberg Variations. Schäuble is said to have invited him in person.

Before his death David Olère left the paintings to Beate and Serge Klarsfeld, who made the prosecution of the perpetrators their life's work. Now Beate Klarsfeld, sitting next to Schäuble, spoke some words of introduction, finishing with the sentence: 'I hope there will be many visitors, including some from the ranks of the AfD members, that they will summon the courage to face up to the works of David Olère and reflect on German identity.'

Igor sits on his piano stool with mixed feelings, delighted at the honour of being allowed to open the exhibition, but he would rather not be here.

Can music, at this moment, make anything better? Or is it a mere shell and ultimately replaceable?

'Of course it matters. But it won't turn an arsehole into less of an arsehole. No one will stand up afterwards and say, oh, I'm the chair of a fascist party, I'm devoted to a reactionary vision of the world and I dream of a right-wing, authoritarian stage – oh, I'm stupid after all. That isn't going to happen, and I have no illusions about it. I'm not claiming that I can turn these guys into better people with music. They'll go on believing what they believe, and they will go on pursuing what they pursue.'

After the last few bars of the aria, Igor, still sitting at the piano, struggles to maintain his silent tension until he can do it no longer. Then he gets to his feet, smiles into the applause, takes his glasses out of the left pocket of his jacket and sits down in the front row.

A brief statement for the parliamentary television channel, and then he steps outside into the morning. By the door he meets another member of parliament who's a friend, and they take a selfie.

Then he writes a tweet. 'I don't know how you all feel, but the idea that Germany in 2020 commemorates the victims of National Socialism in the presence of racists, anti-Semites, neo-fascists and historical relativists brings tears to my eyes.'

He doesn't yet know what to do with the rage he's felt since that morning.

But in fact that's not true.
Of course he knows.

#

One of the things you notice only after you've spent some time in Igor's company is the fact that his expressive ability at the piano is also apparent in another field: he speaks in exactly the same way as he plays the piano.

According to the laws of syntax, sometimes even contrapun-
tally, sometimes improvising and by ear.

With a bit of pedal and the right pauses he can give the most
normal and simple statements in the world an aura as if a great
thought had risen up in him. It doesn't make him any less
sincere; he means exactly what he says.

He can play with tempo and vary the volume: from piano to
fortissimo, back to mezzoforte, then subito piano.

He repeats some sentences several times in a row, sometimes
verbatim, sometimes only retaining the message: 'I have no
barriers. I have none. There are simply none.'

For standard situations in interviews and conversations
he has a repertoire of phrases, little anecdotes, jokes and
big similes ready, which he can conjure from memory at
any time, and which he produces casually in such a way as
to make his listeners believe that they'd only occurred to
him at that moment. A minute later he could repeat them
precisely.

At the same time every word, every pause exactly where it
should be, and it isn't simply reeled off, it's all genuinely felt at
that moment.

Quick sentences are followed by slow ones, ideas that end with
a grand finale, others that simply fade to nothing.

He is also a master of different keys, major and minor in
lightning succession and in various shades, insistently, with
crescendi and accelerandi. He can mark pauses and deliver
punchlines very effectively.

He can improvise over a topic in rondo form, then a phrase is repeated again and again at particular intervals. He speaks in arches, he phases, he reaches the point, sometimes it takes a long time, mostly not.

All quite unconditionally. Every word is weighed. You can't play music indecisively, and Igor can't speak indecisively.

#

Hanover, 6 February 2020, Igor has barely slept, and says by way of greeting: 'Shall we emigrate?' He sounds laconic, exhausted and bitter.

He's sitting in a room under the roof of the Congress Centre in Hanover, after recording the Passacaglia by Ronald Stevenson in the Leibniz Saal two floors below over the past two days.

'I like recording. I like the buzz. I just like sitting there. A recording isn't a solo recital that just happens to have two microphones. It's a world very, very much its own, with its very, very own language and I like that; it's very concentrated and free. I can do what I want a thousand times, I can try out variations, change things, immerse myself. In a way it's incredibly relaxing. And I have enormous fun listening to myself from the side.'

The recording is almost finished; there's just one bar missing. Down in the hall the piano tuner is preparing the grand piano for today's session. You can see it over the monitor. Up here under the roof, Igor's sound editor, Andreas Neubronner – blue pullover, friendly red face, battered jeans, Birkenstocks – has set up a sound booth, and he's clicking through the previous day's work with Igor; they listen to certain passages, and Igor has the score on his knees so that he can check: does everything sound the way it's supposed to, how much softness of tone is ok, what's unacceptable? Like taking a photograph of a large-format painting and then checking it pixel by pixel on the computer. You can't take notes back: in concert they fade away in seconds, even if they're not a perfect fit; in a recording they're there for ever.

But that's not the only thing that concerns Igor. In the regional parliament in the state of Thuringia the previous day, Thomas Kemmerich of the pro-business FDP party was elected governor, with votes from the AfD. That a head of government should have been elected to office with votes from a far-right party had been considered unthinkable until then. Kemmerich accepted the election, but now the political system was taking a look at the situation.

What did the party chairman know? How did the Chancellor react? For how long would the election be valid, and would there be new elections?

'Coffee, Igor?' Neubronner, the sound engineer, asks.
'I've already had three.'
'I think they'll overturn it today', Neubronner says.
'But the genie's out of the bottle.'

Igor, with the score in his lap, taps his phone.
He spent seven hours sitting at the piano the previous day, with horror and bewilderment in between.
'What are we doing with this?' Neubronner asks, clicks, turns the sound up, repeats a passage.
'It's ok. Don't you think?'
'I'm glad you have faith in the Lord.'
'I really don't.'
'Well, faith in the sound engineer, then.'

'Yep.' Igor scrolls through twitter, flicks through the score and scrolls on.

'If there are new elections', Neubronner says, 'the AfD will get more votes than before, I'd bet on it.'

'I'm betting against it, and if I lose I'll boil you up some Käsespätzle.'

'You boil Käsespätzle?'

'Sure! I make the best Käsespätzle in the world! Don't you believe me?'

'You don't boil Käsespätzle, Igor.'

'I don't care.'

Neubronner clicks on; a hugely complicated mass of tracks, frequency curves, amplitudes and digital scraps appears on the monitor.

'Ok, now I'd like to hear bar 165', Igor says. 'Although actually I'd rather not hear it, it's all just loud.'

On they go. One bar, two bars. Another bar. Three bars.

'Yes', Neubronner says, 'it's all fine. Now we'll soon have the worst nightmares behind us.'

The previous evening Igor tweeted: 'I'm never going to forgive any politician, journalist or anybody else who makes a pact with someone whose mid- and long-term political agenda is that someone like me, or anyone else who they declare to be among "the others", should no longer live here.'

Igor goes on flicking through the score. 'Ok, then I'll play the missing bar again. And what else?'

'Just that one bar, Igor.'

'And then everything again?'

'If you like.'

Igor sighs. 'What are we supposed to do now?' It's not clear what he means.

Down in the hall the piano tuner is ready; he can be seen on the monitor getting up and leaving the room.

Igor, excited, looks at his phone. 'Hey, listen to me for a second', then he rattles off a news item: 'After research by *Business Insider* the FDP leadership had decided behind the scenes on electing Kemmerich. On Monday evening, the FDP head for Thüringen phoned Lindner after a meeting of the regional committee. Kemmerich also informs his Party chairman that he is going to go run in the third ballot, if ex-governor Bodo Ramelow (Die Linke) and AfD candidate Christoph Kindervater (Independent) continue to stand. According to information from *Business Insider* the possibility was also discussed that Kemmerich will actually be elected – even with votes from the AfD. According to matching statements from the leadership of the FDP Lindner gave a green light for this.'

Neubronner, dryly: 'Yes, that was clear all along.'

Igor stretches out his arm and holds his mobile under Neubronner's nose, with Twitter open. 'Can I write that here?'

'Yes, of course.'

'Did you read all of it?'

He reads: 'I now say to Christian Lindner: step down, you lack dignity, decency and any kind of political sensitivity. You aren't a liberal. You're an opportunist, you're making a pact with fascists, you're destroying things and setting fires. Step down. Right? So, sent.'

And immediately afterwards: 'Right, then we've got it, then I'll play this now.' He disappears, appears on the monitor a few seconds later and sits down at the piano.

Neubronner gets to his feet, clears up the coffee cups and then says, while Igor records down below, 'I'm a bit worried about him tweeting too much and doing too much. He's an ultra-fast-burner. There are a lot of musicians who've used up all their fuel supplies by the age of 35 or so.'

With his glasses halfway up his nose, he adjusts the tracks on the monitor.

The piano playing from the hall breaks off.

Igor calls, 'Ok?'

Neubronner presses the button on the intercom. Now Igor can hear him in the auditorium like the voice of the Almighty. 'Almost, Igor, I just need one moment.'

And then, quietly, not into the intercom. 'But he can't help it. A few years ago he took a holiday, went to Naples, came back after three days. He couldn't bear it.' And then, into the intercom again:

'So, my friend.'

Igor, in the hall. 'So, top of page 50, right?'

'Exactly.'

'Fine.'

There's already an hour and a half of music in the can, but now comes: the last bar. Neubronner turns on the red light, a sign for: recording in progress.

Igor begins. A rumble in the bass, trills in the descant, fifteen seconds of music, enough lead-up for a small and made-to-measure explosion.

'Ok, then I'll start four bars earlier.'

A powerful crescendo fills the hall, seven seconds, then Igor breaks off. Neubronner, via the intercom: 'That was good!'

Igor, from downstairs: 'Now listen. I'm meeting my mother for dinner in an hour. I can't tell you I'm in a mental state to play the whole thing through again.'

'You don't have to, Igor.'

Igor says something, but Neubronner turns his sound off and speaks himself: 'If you say you don't want to do it any more, then it's enough, we've got what we need. As far as I'm concerned you don't have to.'

Igor says nothing and Neubronner goes on talking. 'If you say you feel a need to play it again, then do it.'

Igor, quietly, from downstairs: 'Well, you said you'd like another version.'

Neubronner, from upstairs: 'If you think you have the strength to get through the piece again, don't worry too much about mistakes.'
'Ok, I'll play the whole piece. I'll play as far as I can get.'
'When do you have to go?'
'In an hour.'
'Right, let's start from the top.'
Red light, quiet please, recording in progress.
Igor plays, Neubronner leans back.
After two and a half minutes he breaks off.
Neubronner, via the intercom: 'Great, see you later, brilliant!'
Igor, from downstairs, quietly. 'Andreas? I can't do it any more.'

'Stop', Neubronner says. 'That's it.' And then, quietly, to himself: 'I knew. Now he's said everything.'

Neubronner turns off the microphone. 'I wouldn't have been able to use it anyway. It had a quite different tempo from the beginning.'

Another question to Igor: how would the recording have gone without the news in the background? – 'Differently' – Did the news fire you up or weigh you down? – 'Weighed me down. How wouldn't it weigh me down?' – Or did the situation also free up some energies? – 'Yes, but I could really do without them.' – Would you be better if these issues weren't there? – 'No, I'd be a different person. But they're just there, and they change my energy.' – How long did you work yesterday? – 'Seven hours. Then we were done and I just lay down on the floor and cried.'

Later he adds that he won't forgive anyone who makes a pact with people who would kill someone like him if they could.

#

The interrupted run-through feels as if Igor, when climbing this mighty peak, had turned round after the first kilometre.

Igor is exhausted, but not content.

It doesn't matter that he was at the peak yesterday, and the day before, that the piece is on tape in various versions, even the problematic passages. Every interruption is an interruption.

Igor, pulling his suitcase on wheels behind him, walks on ahead and calls his manager. He's finished much earlier than planned; he's wasting half a day's studio time, but there was no point going on playing just to use up the time. What if the sound engineer notices that something's missing when cutting and mixing? Then they'll need to book another expensive studio day. His bad conscience plagues him.

Then he turns round.
'That's my old school over there.'

Contrary to what its imperial name suggests, the Kaiser-Wilhelm- und Rats-Gymnasium is not what you would call an imposing piece of architecture.

Igor hasn't been there for ages.

'At some point I just stopped going. Crap marks in Latin, crap marks in science, everything else too.'

He failed his fifth-year exams and, a few months after he entered the Maria Callas Competition, he was held back a year. He felt more at ease in the new class than in the old one, and found friends who he's still in contact with. Nevertheless, a year later, two years before the *Abitur*, the school-leaving exam, he gave up school. 'At the time', he says, 'it was the right decision, but it's not one that I would make again.'

For a few months he regretted dropping out: 'I kept walking from the University of Music to my old school, I went back to class and just sat in. And for a while I thought I'd go back and try it again. But they weren't having it.'

Instead, he threw himself entirely into the piano.

Did he ever dream, in those days, of being where he is now?

'Yes.'

His suitcase clatters so loudly over the cobbles that his voice is almost drowned out.

'That is, no. I never thought in terms of goals, and I don't think that way even today.'

And instead?

'I wanted to practise my Beethoven sonatas, I wanted to talk about the latest Eminem record, I wanted to listen to my Bruckner symphonies. There wasn't much room for anything else. I went through the process that the others were able to go through together, from young teen to young adult, on my own. On the piano stool.'

He played in a series of competitions and came second in all of them: 1998 Ettlingen Piano Competition, 2004 International Maria Callas Competition in Athens, Bad Kissingen Piano Olympics, and a year later the Rubinstein Competition in Tel Aviv. He only came first in Jugend Musiziert. But no one was interested in him, and after each competition he went back to Hanover and continued studying.

There was no career planning in the classic style. There was never a great conductor to sponsor Igor and take him on tour. For a long time there was no agency to feel responsible for Igor.

'The people there all just shrugged. No one was interested in me. So I developed a certain defiance and I said, Fine, then I'll just do what I want. Record companies didn't want me. I was hard to promote, not marketable, odd, a nerd.'

The first attempt with an agency went wrong straight away, and the second failed over four years. It was only when he met his future manager, Kristin Schuster, in the year of his debut with the last five Beethoven sonatas, that he began the part of his life that merits the term 'career'.

'I wanted to grasp the full breadth of music, I always learned too many pieces at once, I went to bits of the repertoire that were unusual for my age: Reger, Hindemith, that was early on. The megalomania came later.'

#

The afternoon after the Stevenson recording on 6 February 2020, on the train from Hanover to Berlin. We were in the dining car, and the plan was to talk about the book. Begin at the beginning. In Hanover or, even better, in Gorki. But what Igor said next immediately made it clear that nothing would come of it. Not now, and not later.

It's a phrase that could put a stop to any book straight away.

'I don't remember me.'

I'm sorry?

'Yes. That's a point that really makes me think. I have the feeling I've been through thirty-three metamorphoses over the last five years alone. I can't tell you what I was like before – I probably haven't even forgotten; I probably never knew. I don't think there's much left of that person.'

Outside the landscape dashes by.

'I don't remember any stories from before, any details or emotions. Not even my voice. I don't even know when the break came. Three years ago, four? A lot has simply gone, to tell the truth.'

More landscape outside.

'I just kept on playing the piano. That was always easy for me, not everything about it, but a lot, and it meant that I didn't have to engage with an awful lot of other things.'

Landscape, landscape, landscape.

'I don't remember Gorki. That's all gone. The stories from those days are the stories of my parents, and if you want to hear those, you'll have to ask them. I have no memory whatsoever of Russia, really nothing at all. Zip. Unfortunately.'

Oh my.

'And I don't remember what I was like as a pupil. I was really bad, I'm clear about that, and I'm sure I was an odd fish. But I wasn't aware of any of that. Who I really am is quite a new question for me.'

Disaster.

'I just got on with my own stuff, with a total focus. I'm very much in the here and today and now. And I also deliberately get rid of some memories. Then I think, I need room for now. If you want to know what I was like before, you'd have to talk to my mother.'

Then we say nothing for a while.

#

To the question of why Igor sounds the way he sounds at the piano, his mother says: 'You hope I can answer this question? I can't. I too am one of the people who wonder that.'

It's the first time Elena Levit has spoken publicly about her son.

'I've had requests. And I'm supposed to say sweet things about my little Igor? He was never a sweet child. And I was never a sweet Mama. And I made mistakes too. The last 33 years in my life are actually a bit of a mystery to me.'

In Gorki, Elena Levit studied piano with Berta Marantz, an authority whose piano classes were among the best in Russia. She in turn was a former pupil of Genrich Gustavovich Nejgauz, Germanized name: Heinrich Neuhaus.

Elena Levit first ran the piano department at the Music School for Children and Young People in Gorki, and worked as a repetiteur and lecturer in the conducting class at the University of Music. She now teaches in Hanover.

She asks: 'Does he remember his childhood?'
No.
'Then he's like me', she says. 'I remember – and it may be unconscious – only the things that I experienced as emotionally very, very beautiful. A lot that made me unhappy has disappeared. We have a difficult journey behind us. But you know what they say: Every moment that we experience as misfortune can turn out to be good fortune in retrospect. I'm grateful for everything we've experienced. Even if it was often not easy.'

In Gorki Igor's parents lived in a tiny apartment in a low-rise block on the outskirts of the city. Buildings thrown up quickly so that people had somewhere to live.

Her father gave her a piano as a wedding present. The living room, with an area of thirteen square metres, was too small for a grand piano, and in any case there wouldn't have been enough money for one. The couple had a daughter, and six years later a son.

Even during her pregnancy Elena travelled as a repetiteur to conducting competitions, and no one was supposed to know that she was pregnant, because otherwise she wouldn't have been able to go. She managed to keep Igor secret for a long time. Later she took him with her, and he slept under the grand piano in the conductor's room.

\#

At the age of two Igor ran to the piano, sang the tune from a Russian cartoon and tried to accompany himself. Hour after hour, day after day. He effortlessly copied everything that he heard. 'He drove us mad', his mother says.

At home they never set themselves the goal of turning the child into a musical genius. 'He actually forced us.' When he was three and a half, mother and son started piano lessons.

Elena Levit took Igor along to the conservatoire for early-years classes. The parents of other children complained that Igor was too impatient: he called out the answers in class. Igor's parents got a letter and Igor was thrown out.

Elena heard of a class in the University of Music that her colleagues' children attended. The director called Elena in a few weeks later and said, 'Take him out. Do it privately, it's pointless here.'

Elena introduced Igor to her friend Irina Sarafians, barely older than she was herself, who taught at the School of Music.

'We were always worried that we'd over-teach him. He was such an independent child. I knew from experience.'

Irina Sarafians started teaching him at the School of Music. Elena Levit at home. For a long time he had been playing pieces that he shouldn't have been able to play at his age. His mother says today: 'It was a very enjoyable time.'

Piano lessons for children were highly regulated at the time. Which pieces were to be taught in the first class, which in the second, and in between exams to see how the students were developing. If a child was particularly gifted, they were able to deviate from the rigid timetable. But there was a framework, and they had to stay within that framework: 'And I was worried about that – about that strict framework and rules. I can adapt, I know, I'm older. He would have rebelled, he wouldn't have gone along with it.'

He was allowed free access at the University of Music; his mother put a few coins in his pocket and he went to the canteen and got served. He saw the whole of the University of Music as his own private hunting ground, and everyone knew him. The doorman knew that Igor was allowed to go anywhere, but not out.

When he was three years old his mother introduced him to her own professor, Berta Marantz. Igor played a Bach invention, and his mother was annoyed because he used the wrong fingering. She said only: 'Mrs Marantz, he's three years old! There is nothing I can do! He plays until he runs out of fingers, and then he just turns his hand round.'

He played the way it suited him. And when his mother said, please stick to the fingering, he said: Don't look!

Her colleagues had much more belief in him than she did herself. 'I had my doubts, for a very long time, about whether the musician's life was really the right thing.'

At the age of six he played his first concerto with an orchestra: the concerto for organ and orchestra in F major by Georg Friedrich Handel, nicknamed: *The Cuckoo and the Nightingale*. It was winter, and his mother was worried that he would catch cold. He wore a thick pullover under his white shirt. He was very small and thin for his age.

The only person who was nervous was his mother. It was an important concert; you have to concentrate, she said. He replied: But you're here, you do it.

At the age of seven Igor played the graduation concert at his school of music. His mother sent him to an old lady to teach him the theory of harmony, so that he wasn't just playing notes off the page but understood how harmonies came together. And she sent him for aural training. 'He didn't need that; he only needed to know the terms. He needed the names for what he was hearing.'

Then, almost overnight, Irina Sarafians emigrated. Her husband was a pianist, and he got a job in Croatia. 'That was a crisis for me', Igor's mother says. 'But now I had to be strong as well. That was the point when I stopped being Mama in his lessons.'

#

And then the decision was made to leave Russia. 'I knew we had to do something for Igor.' The question was: to Moscow? Or even further?

'We wouldn't have coped with Moscow, not least because of the mentality. That way of thinking in terms of athletic performance – I was always worried that Igor would be under that kind of pressure.'

What would that have meant? 'No idea, I still can't quite define it. I was just worried. Perhaps that way would have been much easier for us too.'

The situation in Russia was politically and economically unstable. No wages had been paid for months at the University of Music, and it didn't occur to anyone to stop teaching. Elena's colleagues were working four hours a week and weren't being paid, Elena herself two and three times as much. Igor's father Simon was a construction engineer, working as a senior foreman. But there wasn't much building going on.

'We wouldn't have left if it hadn't been for the children. We had secure jobs, and if it had only been about us, we'd have stayed. But we knew we were young and strong; we'd get through it.'

Igor's mother sent a recording of Igor's piano-playing to Professor Vladimir Krainev, who taught in Hanover. Krainev listened to the tape and invited the family to the city.

That was the sign she had hoped for.
Now there was no turning back.

Elena tried to keep a clear head, to sort out what was important and what wasn't.

When she came home from the Conservatoire that evening, everything was gone.

'I'm grateful to my husband for that. He just sorted out everything, so it wouldn't be as painful for me. The books were left, the scores as well, Russian classics, which were very important to me. We gradually brought them to Germany.'

#

On 4 December 1995 Elena, Simon, Alla and Igor Levit arrived at Düsseldorf Airport. As they were coming in to land, Igor saw the tower with the radar turning on it and said to his sister: 'Look, this is where we live now.'

So that was how the new life began, and it started with a five-mark note. The family was standing in Düsseldorf Airport and needed a luggage trolley. For the luggage trolley they needed a one-mark coin.

But the words needed to change the note into coins had vanished. Simon Levit tried to give a woman the note so that she would give him her trolley. She didn't understand what he wanted; he talked away at her, she gave him a coin, he reached for the trolley and she started shouting. 'It went on until I recovered and found the word "change" in my head,' Elena Levit says. 'A very funny beginning, very difficult.'

The family came to the country as Jewish quota refugees.

She moved in with Simon's mother, who had left Russia a year before and lived in Dortmund.

It took me a few years before I stopped looking back. We arrived quite quickly, and I managed not to be nostalgic. The children helped us look forward, and I'm very grateful for that. But even so, it was a long journey.' Igor attended primary school, and received a lot of support and encouragement from the teacher.

For the first few months a Russian-speaking classmate helped him translate. 'We pressed the reset button on our lives.'

None of them spoke German. Elena had done thorough prepa-ration and learned grammar – 'but the practical side of things, when you constantly have the language around you: that's not easy.'

In the spring of 1996, the family went to Hanover. Elena Levit worked as a babysitter, taught early-years music classes at kindergarten and learned the language from the children. 'I wasn't worried about making mistakes in front of them. With grown-ups it was harder – I wanted to be correct, so I said nothing. With the little ones: no problem. The children are much more generous.'

It took Igor's father a long time to find his feet professionally. 'I got work quickly, but it took a long time before I was where I was happy. I started right at the bottom in the construction industry. On my first work contract it said: assistant.'

Igor's sister Alla was 13, and she went straight to the *Gymnasium*, to grammar school.

Mother and daughter spent whole afternoons sitting on the living-room floor with the dictionary and the history book, and wept. It was about the Napoleonic Wars, and they both knew all the details in Russian, but in German they didn't understand a word. But the school had a music department, and there was also a Russian class that helped. 'You jump into cold water, you cry for a few months, then it gets better.' After five years she passed the *Abitur* with a solid 2.0.
She gave up playing the piano.
'She played very well. She could have studied.'
But one day she told her mother that she didn't want to be an average pianist.

\#

One day Igor came home from school and said he would soon speak better German than all his classmates. The reason was ambition, but not just that. He was at a good school, but he didn't wear branded clothes, and his classmates called him the 'dosser child'.

'Children are sometimes brutal. Deliberately or otherwise. It's normal. I know that today, but I didn't at the time. I think Igor was hurt quite often.'

By the spring after their move, Igor's German was almost flawless. He was the only one who answered the phone at home, and at the age of eight or nine he was dealing with all the family's affairs. 'I don't know what he told them', his mother says and laughs, 'but we're still alive.'

He acted as his father's interpreter at parents' evening. 'Herr Levit, we have discussed everything with your son, I'm glad you agree', the teacher said, 'please sign here.' She handed him a piece of paper. His father asked: 'What's this?' Igor said: 'Oh, you can sign that, it's all fine.' It was permission to look after the class guinea pigs over the summer holidays, and for the next few weeks a huge cage stood in the family's kitchen.

His time in fifth and sixth years were unhappy for Igor. The teachers couldn't tell what a quick thinker he was; he felt he wasn't being seen – and he wasn't mistaken.

'We hadn't quite worked things out', his mother says, 'not in terms of language, and not in terms of understanding the mentality.'

He was pegged as a failure. He got bad marks, he froze, he simply stopped joining in. But rather than asking why he had frozen, he was given one fail after another. He still managed to get into *Gymnasium*. He wasn't a successful pupil, but the class clown, who gets bad marks.

He didn't take a great interest in school. In some subjects he only had a single exercise book for years. On the front it says: Igor Levit, sixth year. Then that's crossed out, and above it: seventh class. Crossed out: eighth class. His mother later found the exercise book in the attic, and he said: Look how thrifty I am.

When he was supposed to write an essay, he would stop after a paragraph. He thought there was nothing more to be said. His mother said: You could just have written another few sentences about, I don't know, the blue sky. He replied: I don't understand what's supposed to be missing. Bottom marks.

'In spite of the whole thing I learned a lot', his mother said. 'Never in my life would I dare to say about a student: he's talentless, he won't make anything of himself. Never in my life. You simply had to rely on the energy materializing out of somewhere. You just had to allow him to develop. In retrospect that's clear, but while it was happening?'

#

In the spring of 2004, at the age of 17, Igor entered the Maria Callas Competition in Athens, and played a massive programme of seven piano concertos. He came second. When he got home, he found out that he hadn't passed the school year.

'I don't know what was wrong, and I was worried about going in: I was worried that people would say things to me that I wouldn't know how to deal with. It was difficult. Because I knew that I couldn't change anything at home.'

Igor had actually promised to his mother to make an effort and jump a year. Now he says: I did make a jump. But in the wrong direction.

'What should I have done?' Elena Levit says. 'Scream? Cause a fuss? Issue prohibitions? We just had to get through it. Of course that took a lot of strength. But he also knew he had us on his side.'

He repeated the year, and now a happy time began; he met new people and formed some friendships that have lasted up to today.

He didn't decide to drop out of school overnight; in fact he didn't decide at all. He just stopped going.

#

'I have a feeling that he is never contented, and he's lucky that way', his mother says. 'He's always hungry, and that's good, even if it makes him feel uneasy and unhappy for a while.'

Sometimes Igor says to his mother before a concert: Please don't come.

'We're not hurt when he says that. There are days when I know myself: Let's not go. I'm tense, not about Igor's playing, but because it'll be stressful before the concert and after. I'll make a fuss. So we stay home.'

He has great self-doubt, his mother says. 'It's a great benefit. I say, Igor, it's so good to have that. There are enough people who know it all in advance.'

#

Igor's career also required an excessive degree of self-esteem. The idea of recording all the Beethoven sonatas is a good example of that, and the idea is older than Igor's recording contract. Michael Becker, the director of the Düsseldorf Tonhalle, asked him, after a concert in 2010, whether he fancied doing it. At the time, out of the thirty-two sonatas, Igor could only play five.

'I just said: Yes of course, it's not that much work.' It took him a year to learn the rest, he says.

He went to his teacher, Matti Raekallio, and told him he'd just received his first offer: a recording of all the Beethoven sonatas. Raekallio, who had also played the sonata cycle decades before, leapt to his feet and shouted: 'This is amazing!' Igor said, 'Come on, how long can it take?'

It took almost five years.

Igor deferred the start of recordings four times – the plan was for a date in the 2011/12 season, whereas it didn't actually happen until the 2015/16 season.

When he made his record deal with Sony in 2013, the programme he wanted to record had already been in place for years.

Igor has an eye for a good opportunity. And when he spots a chance, it becomes more important than anything else.

In the late summer of 2010, a call came in from Weimar: the pianist Boris Berezovsky, who was supposed to be playing the 'Études d'exécution transcendante' by Franz Liszt, had to cancel. Could Igor take over?
Yes, Igor said. Was he familiar with the Études? Yes.

He told his mother he'd been approached to step in for Berezovsky.

'But if you step in, you'll have to suggest a programme.'
'I'm playing the Liszt Études.'
'You don't know them.'
'I've already said yes.'

Igor only knew half of Étude No. 9, a bit of No. 10, Nos. 11 and 12 not at all.

'I'm like this, that the crazier a situation becomes, the calmer I am. I mean, should I have turned it down?'

The call came in a day and a half before the concert. Igor had a day and a night to learn the remaining four pieces – and they aren't the easiest ones in the cycle.

'So I sat down and learned them. I knew I could do it. I was a hundred per cent sure.'

And then?

'Then I went to Weimar and played them. I won't tell you where, but there have been a few concerts like that in my life. When I feel it's worth it, I can't guarantee that I won't do it again. I don't care how much effort it takes, all that matters is the moment I'm working towards.'

Igor's mother, at home in Hanover, was ready to call the police – she hadn't heard anything from her son since the day before the concert. Of course it must have been a disaster, of course he must have overreached himself and misjudged the whole thing and now he didn't dare to call her.

The next day he called.
'How did it go?'
'Oh, brilliantly. The reviews are quite good too.'

'But you didn't know half the pieces.'
'I had a few hours before the concert.'

Igor's debut in the Golden Hall of the Vienna Musikverein was one such story. On the morning of Monday, 16 June 2014, Igor himself didn't know he would be performing that evening in Vienna. At lunchtime he was in a café in Hanover having a piece of apricot cake when his phone rang: Maurizio Pollini had just pulled out of the recital, and could he take his place? The concert started at 7.30 pm, there was a flight, he would land in Vienna at 6.00 pm and be brought straight to the concert hall. Igor agreed, on two conditions: he needed a black bow tie, because he had lost his own. And he would play whatever he liked. Then he set off for the airport. At 7.30 pm he stepped onto the podium of the Golden Hall, played the Beethoven sonatas Opus 110 and Opus 111, and in the second half 'The People United Will Never Be Defeated!' In his address the director asked the audience to please stick around after the interval.

\#

Igor's demands on concert tours, compared with those of many colleagues, are rather modest.

'I'm completely uncomplicated. I don't want baskets of fruit backstage. I used to want two bananas, now I don't even want those. If I do find a fruit basket, I have to eat the whole thing so that it's gone, otherwise it gets on my nerves. Just give me a couple of bottles of water, and we're fine.

There's just one thing: I would like round-the-clock access to a piano – it doesn't matter what kind, a rehearsal piano backstage is fine. I want to be able to work all the time. I sit at the piano much more when I'm travelling than I do at home.

What else am I supposed to do? I'm on my own. I find going to museums on my own sad – who am I supposed to talk to about what I see there?

And I'd like a small hotel room. Please not a big one – big rooms make me nervous, because I have the feeling I'm always losing something. Under no circumstances two rooms – that's an absolute horror as far as I'm concerned. But there are small rooms; the nicest hotels have the nicest small rooms. A table, a wardrobe, a bed, that's it. And not too big a bed, or I feel small. I have the feeling it isn't all for me; I haven't deserved it.

If someone says to me before the concert: Sorry, we don't have a hotel room for you, please sleep on the couch in the green room – it's not a problem. And if there's nothing to eat there apart from a bag of nuts and raisins, that's ok too. The only thing I would like is a good cup of coffee in the morning.

It's the same if there are other people there too. It's easier for me to be generous towards people I like than towards myself. I don't have strong feelings about money either. As long as I have some, I spend it – with very few exceptions – on other people. I invite them, I muck in, help, get involved. With other people I like to have a great meal and then find some brilliant bar to go to. But not alone. When I'm travelling or teaching in Hanover, I go to the sushi stall at the station or the Korean next door. I grab a spring roll, eat it and go. I don't differentiate between work and leisure; it's all the same. I'm not keen on having free time when I'm alone. When I'm with somebody else, then always.

When I feel really secure, I don't care about my phone. I don't care about concerts. I don't care about my career. I can turn it off like a light, and everything's a blank. When I'm alone, I can't do that.'

#

When he was studying, Igor concentrated on the subjects that interested him. He took piano lessons, but seldom went to lectures. Instead, he put all his efforts into the exams. He didn't see them as a test of his achievements, but as the opportunity to present his ideas.

'I just like learning. I enjoyed thinking up concepts and showing what happened to be there. And I was always coming up with these particularly offbeat things.'

When other people were playing Bach, he was playing Frescobaldi, just because he could. He decided to learn a piece by Max Reger – 'lots of people are deaf to Reger' – and then used every opportunity to play the piece.

When his fellow students were practising for piano concertos, Igor would play the orchestra part on a second piano. Sometimes six or seven hours on a single piece. He did the same when taking classes with other professors that he got on well with.

He wanted to use every opportunity to show what he could do in front of an audience. 'In front of two people, three people, even now it's exactly the same. I like to have a really good acoustic, but in the end I don't care. I also like a really good grand piano, but I can play on any old crate. The main thing is that there are people in the hall that I can show something to.'

Other pianists can speak for hours about which piano in which hall sounds good for the pieces of which composer – Igor just shrugs. But not out of general indifference. He's impelled by something else. It's not the desire to deliver a perfect interpretation, probed precisely in advance, of the piece listed in the programme.

'When I play a piano concerto, I'm not interested in whether the orchestra might be too loud or the woodwind are playing too quietly. It may be a very odd idea, but – I'm not going on stage for my own sake, but for the sake of the people in the auditorium. Because I want to show them something – and give them something. Those things are ten thousand times more important to me than a perfect grand piano in a perfect acoustic setting.'

\#

Is there an ideal moment for each work in the life of a pianist? The right degree of maturity? And if there is, who makes the call? Would it sometimes be good if someone said: wait, it's too soon for this one?

'Meaning what? Who for? Tell me, who for? Who has the right to tell a free human being what they are able to do or not?'

Igor mentions Dong Ping, a 17-year-old Chinese student of his at the University in Hanover. 'If he feels like playing the Hammerklavier Sonata or the B minor sonata by Franz Liszt – please go ahead! I'll insist on it. But it'll only make him grow. If, along the way, I get the feeling that it's too much for him emotionally or mentally, then I'll say straight away: ok, hold fire, it's too much. But I won't stop him having a go.'

It has often happened to him, Igor says, that thoughts and above all feelings have overtaken hands.

'If you can play everything but it all turns into chaos and you're gasping for breath because you're overflowing with feelings and your emotions are running away with you – that's the best thing that can happen to you.'

What can you do to dam this flood of emotions?

'Don't ask me. I've always been like that. I have no barriers.

No, I tell him: you will practise that very slowly now for three months. Very slowly. Of course he won't. I didn't either. But that's what I tell him. And then we get to work.

I don't need to teach him how to play the piano. I just need to teach him how to make deliberate decisions. I didn't know how to do that at 17 either.

I give him pieces to listen to – basically I'm doing with him what I did off my own bat. I tell him: in the B Minor Mass there's this one aria, and there's that one phrase in it, that one word, that's exactly like your piece. What do you think of that? Do you notice? Ok, then do what you like with it; I'm just trying to draw your attention to it.'

The goal is not a presentation of the work that is true to the original.
The goal is for the pianist to make the piece his own. To tell his own story.

In the classical sphere, which consists entirely of rules, conventions and traditions, right and wrong, that's something completely new.

'Rachmaninov suffered that way when he did this or that – we all know those stories. Let it go. Sure, there will be people in the audience who don't know. That's what Wikipedia's for. I see my role differently. I'm telling my story, my own, the one that's closest to my heart. The information about what happened to this piece 100, 200, 300 years ago isn't really any business of mine.'

#

Friday, 7 February 2020, the day after the Stevenson recording. We've arranged to meet at Café Einstein Unter den Linden. An hour before we're due to meet Igor writes: 'I'm already there.' The night before he could hardly sleep, at about 11 at night he took a stroll to the Dussmann bookshop on Friedrichstrasse, took a pile of books to the till, then changed his mind and took all the books back again.

He is sitting below a series of portraits of politicians:
Helmut Kohl in front of the Capitol in Washington.
Johannes Rau hugging Gerhard Schröder.
A reflective Willy Brandt in close-up.
Helmut Schmidt playing chess.
Igor wonders whether he should order something to eat here, or later somewhere else.

That's another question.

– After all the discussions of the past few weeks, after all the doubting and not knowing where to go next. Could it be that you're about to give up your career as a solo pianist?

Igor laughs.

– I don't think so. I do think, though, that I'm going to play substantially less.

– Why don't you stop?

– A lot would have to happen to make me stop. To keep me
from sleeping at night. Something would have to happen in
politics or society that meant I couldn't do it any more. No, I'm
not going to stop. But I won't go on living at the same rhythm
as I am at the moment.

– Is the career part of your life a bit too much about you?

– It is partly about me. The point is very simple. It makes
me very happy not to be alone. But I'm constantly alone as a
pianist.

– So where does it go from here?

– No idea. I wouldn't have seen myself here a year ago. Or
even six months ago. But ideally I'd like everything to be
different tomorrow. In my head I'm ten kilometres further on
than my concert diary. Because I feel different from the way
I felt three years ago when we filled the diary. My head and
my development are overtaking my lived reality at full speed.
That's not easy. I'm a professional and not a bad person, so I
don't throw everything overboard. In my inner development I
turn around faster and faster and get clearer and clearer, but
this reality remains fixed as it is, and I would like to have it
different already. I want something from my life that my life
can't give me.

Igor has had enough. He wants to go home. Not here and now,
but in general. He notices a powerful urge to retreat. Have
some time, meet up with friends, not hastily and by chance,
but just normally. And finally, finally not to be exhausted any
more.

'Now I have it, now I have the answer: I would like my everyday life to be as changeable as I am. I would like it to change simply from day to day. But on the contrary, I plan my concerts three years in advance. And I like performing them. The concerts don't put me in a different mood; it's a different level. But right now I'm changing so much, faster than my life allows – because my life isn't changing at all, and that really annoys me.'

#

Elena Levit had enough foresight to put her son in the hands of a second teacher. It's never a good idea to be Mama and the only teacher at the same time.

'We said to ourselves, let's take this path', she says, 'and if the Lord God determined this path for Igor, then that's how it's to be. But please don't do it by force. Force doesn't work.'

But she's still involved, even today. 'I no longer perform, but of course we exchange ideas, we talk all the time', Igor says. 'I've copied a lot from her in my teaching, so we're colleagues now.'

His mother leaves him in peace. He's allowed to do what he likes, but not how he likes.

Her principle: you can have the best idea in the world about how the piece you're playing should sound – it won't be any good if you lack the craft to let it become true.

'She criticized me very, very harshly, time and again. She never said: you can't play this piece, you can't do it this way. It was always: what do you want, and when you did what you did, was it the right way?'

It's not only a matter of the difference between right and wrong notes, but about sound, technique, balance. How do you make a note sound the way you imagine it? Every tempo affects the balance of the piece. To play forte, you need to know what piano sounds like.

That means trying out, building, testing, rejecting for hours, weeks at a time.

The goal: technical superiority, not so much over other pianists as over the dangers of the piece.

Hold your wrist like that, not like that.
Bend your fingers more.
Even more!

#

Apart from three private lessons, Vladimir Krainev, on whose invitation the Levit family came to Hanover in 1994, never taught Igor himself. Igor was still too young.

He sent him instead to his colleague Julia Goldstein, who taught children and young people. Her father was a famous Soviet violinist, while her husband at the time, the pianist Wolfgang Manz, studied with Karl-Heinz Kämmerling. Igor was nine years old when he started lessons with Julia Goldstein, and he stayed with her for three years.

'I can't remember what we worked on. But it was three very important years. I hold her in very high esteem.'

In 1998 Igor entered the International Competition for young pianists in Ettlingen. His year group also included his colleague Yuja Wang. Igor took second prize, Yuja Wang third, while the winner was Boris Giltburg from Israel, three years older than Igor.

On the jury was Hans Leygraf, nearly 80, with a beard and kind eyes. After an active concert career, he was a professor of piano in Hanover and Salzburg. Long-since retired, he still ran a piano class for gifted international students in Salzburg.

Leygraf invited Igor onto a course that he was about to give in Darmstadt, and the distinction was almost greater than second prize in the competition. Igor and his mother went there, and Julia Goldstein, when she found out about it, was not exactly free of jealousy, an emotion far from unknown to most teachers. In Darmstadt, Leygraf told Igor he should apply as a young student to the Mozarteum in Salzburg, and he would happily accept him into his gifted class.

His mother smoothed the way with Julia Goldstein for him.

In Hanover Karl-Heinz Kämmerling asked Elena Levit if she would allow him to teach her son. She declined.

Then Igor travelled with his mother to Salzburg to sit the entrance exam. Five hours by train to Munich, the next day on to Salzburg. They spent the night on the floor at the home of some acquaintances in the suburb of Neuperlach-Süd.

The next day Igor sat the entrance exam in the Viennese Hall of the Mozarteum, and hasn't a clue what pieces he played.

The consideration of the commission went on for hours, with Igor and his mother waiting outside the hall. Eventually the door opened and Leygraf said simply: You're in.

He immediately gave Igor some big pieces to do. Grieg's Concerto in A minor, Beethoven's Sonata Opus 26, no treatments or transcriptions – core repertoire.

'Basically that class was more important psychologically than pianistically', Igor says. 'Leygraf was a formative personality for me. An important, very well-known teacher. I was at a university for the first time, in Salzburg for the first time, at the Mozarteum – even that was very important to me.'

'That was a special friendship: Igor, eleven at the time, and Leygraf, 80. I don't know how Igor would have developed without those two years with Leygraf', Elena Levit says. 'He's just an artist, also a teacher, yes, but above all an artist. A person with incredible intelligence. They played billiards together, told jokes. Igor also travelled on his own with Leygraf; he became much more confident, more self-reliant.'

Once again it was about craft and physical posture, but his body changed ten times anyway, and by the age of 14 everything was different.

'I sat in the room, in the class; those were times when I was still playing the piano-mother. Leygraf taught Igor for sometimes five or six hours. And I knew that Igor couldn't keep going for more than two hours. He looked out the window, he asked silly questions and I thought: What are you doing, I've travelled across the whole country, and now you're talking nonsense. But it was exactly the right thing at that time. It was exactly what Igor needed at the time: friendship with that man, who had stayed young, and who treated Igor with great respect. That friendship was exactly what Igor needed.'

In the other weeks his mother was the teacher. 'I didn't teach him, I accompanied him', she says. 'I tried to teach him to understand what he could see. Just open the doors on the text, on what he was reading there. To read, to recognize. Because there are very, very many who have great motor training but no idea what they're playing. I experience that every day.'

The classes were held at home, and more than once the lunch got burnt because there was a problem to be solved on the piano. 'I was the only person who accompanied him professionally, but I have never had his talent, never. I went on that journey together with Igor, I learned most of it at the same time as he did. I don't know if Igor's aware of that. I grew pianistically along with Igor.'

A lot of people have stuck their oar in to influence the way Igor plays, giving him good and bad advice. 'He was able to tell the difference, he could do that, I couldn't', his mother said. 'He was much, much stronger than me in that respect.'

Spending a few years living only for practice, doing nothing but practise and investing in the future and otherwise having no life: that's not on. 'No. But you can see that, you can hear that', Igor's mother says. 'And perhaps that's the reason why he sounds the way he does.

'He practised as much as he needed to. And it took me some time to understand that. But he did all kinds of other nonsense. He developed perfectly normally: with computer games, with bad marks at school, it was all there.'

Igor practises lying in bed, but hearing things in his head. 'At first I used to get very upset about that', his mother says. 'But it's just part of his gift, which I don't have. He reads the score, he works with it, and I've always had the feeling that by the time he gets to the piano he knows it by heart.'

#

For a year Igor and his mother spent weekends commuting from Hanover to Salzburg. The prize money from Ettlingen was used up quite quickly; the regular journeys were far beyond the family's means, and soon beyond their strength as well. Somehow it worked anyway. 'It was a beautiful and an incredibly difficult time', Igor says.

And then it stopped working.

'We needed lessons here in Hanover; we slowly had to get back to normality', his mother says. 'I had to work, I couldn't go with Igor any more, and I couldn't afford it financially either.'

In Hanover Martin Brauss and Bernd Goetzke established an Institute for the Early Promotion of the Musically Gifted. Igor joined in the first year and finally, at the age of 13, became a student with Karl-Heinz Kämmerling.

Kämmerling, only ten years younger than Leygraf, no beard but an artist's white mane, was one of the piano world's luminaries; without exaggeration he was one of the most successful piano teachers in the world. He taught for over 50 years. And that was also the aura that he built up around himself. 'He turned himself into a brand', Igor says. 'Quite rightly.'

Kämmerling himself is not a concert pianist, but his students include some big names – Wolfgang Manz, Alice Sara Ott, Sophie Pacini, Herbert Schuch, Lars Vogt, and also a number of future piano professors.

And he knows that too.

Igor studied with Kämmerling for five years, between the ages of 13 and 18, a formative time but not an easy one. 'We had', Igor says, 'our disagreements.'

From Kämmerling Igor learned discipline and precision. 'A brilliant man, he simply has the ear, the head and the nose for talent', Igor's mother says.

Kämmerling was a teacher with aura and an instinct for power, incredibly solicitous, but with an iron fist, and known among his students as a dictator, about whom it is said: There are things that you will only learn from him.

'He was extremely rigid about sticking to rules and principles. He had his templates, his basic exercises, his ideas of tempo, his precise metronomic instructions. He applied them to everything. If you had a problem with the arpeggio in the left hand, there was exactly one way to practise it – because that's how you do it. He trained very different personalities, but his methods were always the same. And that's fine. You're at the age when you need to learn some vocabulary. And he taught you vocabulary.'

Kämmerling himself couldn't keep up with his pupils in pianistic terms, but he made sure that their playing improved, simply rolling his office chair up to the piano and sitting down next to them.

'He was a psychological genius. He trained you to be a pianist without really being one himself. He insisted. He taught me how to work. And I worked on this one Beethoven sonata with him, Opus 2 No. 2, seven thousand five hundred and fifty-five billion times; we played the same passages, over and over and over again. He kept talking about an imprint in the brain that's been pressed there and stayed. And I've applied that method to lots of other pieces.'

The climatic conditions between them were changeable, alternating between sunny intervals and violent showers, often without transition.

'He also had his dark side. He was incredibly jealous. You couldn't even look at other teachers out of the corner of your eye. I remember him saying to me: "The people who turned into something with me were the ones who danced only to my tune." And, sorry, that just doesn't work with everybody. At age 16, 17 we had our first disagreements. I showed up with my Bruckner symphonies and he said: You're just going to turn into a conductor.

'Then I showed up with something else and he rolled his eyes. I wanted to play Rachmaninov's Corelli Variations, and he put me right off them; it's a piece I will never touch again. He roared his head off at me. He said in front of other people that my playing had been, quote, shit. That does something to you as a sixteen-year-old. There were very, very fierce arguments. He always liked me, no question. But he was unbelievably protectionist.'

In the most important competitions in the world Kämmerling was on the jury, and every pianist knew: If he doesn't think highly of you, you can basically kiss your career goodbye.

The pressure that Kämmerling built up was incredibly high, and he was hard to get away from. Masterclasses with other teachers were seen as a breach of trust, and he made his mark through his students, focusing on individuals because he thought they were going to be the new Pollini. He said to other students: Anyway, you're not as good as this one or that one.

'He was a chess player, brilliant, but cruel', Igor says. 'A great pedagogue, a great teacher, someone who played an essential role in my life, but who like all people had a very dark side and who made me suffer a very great deal.'

'Igor and Kämmerling weren't a good fit', Igor's mother says. 'And it was very important for Igor to notice that it wasn't working.'

#

At around this time Igor started to feel frustrated.

He was finding the piano limiting. For a long time he had felt misunderstood; he couldn't express himself, which disturbed him.

More than ever he wanted to do more than just play the piano. And he was completely terrified.

'I never showed it, but I was very tense. I wanted something else and I couldn't have it, because I didn't know what it was.'

He was discontented with himself, with his body; he weighed nearly seventeen stone, he was getting bad marks at school, but the crisis was manifested at the piano.

'I didn't feel like it any more – I've always played the piano, and I'd stopped wanting to do it. I felt misunderstood and unseen.

'I had the feeling that all of my studies were based on that little word "one", and on rules about all the things *one* should do and the things that *one* mustn't do. I wanted to know what I wanted to do. I wanted to speak differently, learn different things.

'I never showed it to anyone, but deep inside I was actually on the way down.'

Then a new phase began, in which Igor learned a huge amount of repertoire, not only the very specific piano repertoire, but everything he could get hold of, including operas, Wagner and even Bruckner.

In Salzburg, again at one of Kämmerling's summer schools, his colleague Herbert Schuch showed him a recording of Anton Bruckner's Symphony No. 8, with Sergiu Celibidache and the Munich Philharmonic.

Igor succumbed completely to the music, and listened only to that one symphony. Then he discovered Symphony No. 7 and only listened to that one.

'I devoured that music; I was incredibly moved by it. I started spreading my wings. And Kämmerling didn't know what to do. I simply went in a different direction from the one he had planned for me.

'Then came the Max Reger phase, later Hindemith, then Wagner – it was simply expansive, big, long. And bigger than the piano: eighty-eight keys wasn't enough to grasp it. I was incredibly fascinated by it.'

#

At the age of 17, Igor went to Martin Brauss, the director of the Institute for the Early Promotion of the Musically Gifted, and said: Dear Martin, I hate my instrument. I can't do it any more. Brauss sent him to Lajos Rovatkay, emeritus Professor at the university and an expert in fifteenth-century Franco-Flemish polyphony.

Back to the beginning of the Western musical tradition. Tabula rasa.

Lajos Rovatkay lived very nearby. Igor paid him a visit and Rovatkay greeted him with the question: Do you know Josquin?

Igor said no. Rovatkay talked himself into a rage – how is that possible? Do people at University learn nothing at all these days? Why do all pianists only want to play Bach, only ever Bach, when Bach is unthinkable without Josquin? Why do teachers not teach their pupils phrasing any more? You learn phrasing better from Josquin than from anyone else. That kind of thing.

Rovatkay had fled Hungary, come to Germany via Vienna, studied in Frankfurt and then moved to Hanover.

'He's spectacular. There's something Beethovenesque about him, something wild. But so clever, so inspired and so young, so incredibly young.' He was the man with whom Igor once again learned a completely new way of playing the piano.

Igor started taking lessons from Rovatkay. 'We listened to an amazing amount of music. He has a way of teaching that also told me a lot about myself.

'One example: I played a little Bach invention. He said: "That's so wonderful, so wonderful, I mean, how many people play that the way you do? I just have one small question." And then four and a half hours pass, and there's nothing whatsoever left of me. And then he says to me: "Wonderful, and now please play it badly again, the way you did at the beginning." I tried, and it was bloody hard, to play it deliberately badly. But it's a useful piece of instruction: you have to learn where you come from and where you've been. You don't just go home because the lesson's over, you try to imagine very clearly: where did I start, what happened.'

And what happened in the four and a half hours in between?

'I play the first six notes. Da-da-da-da-da-da … he says: "Wonderful, wonderful, but what would it sound like if I picked up my bow and played that passage on the violin? Then the first note would have a little accent." I play: Yaaa-da-da-da-da-da… "Yes Yes! But not so flat, the first note is more exalted, not so flat, more passion, but only on the first note." Yaaa-da-da-da-da-da-da… "Wait, do you know the passage in that motet by Schütz, I'll just show it to you" – and we spend almost half an hour getting the distance between the first and the second note exactly right. Then I play: Yaaa-da-da-da-da-da-doo-di-di-di, and he breaks in: "Why legato? You're playing Yaaa-da-da-da-da-da-doo-di-di-di, but in the score it says Yaaa-da-da-da-da-da doo di-di-di, with two little breath marks." Then we talked for an hour about how Philipp Emanuel Bach speaks about breath marks in his book about the art of keyboard playing, and Leopold Mozart about breath marks on the violin. So we experiment about how to play breath marks correctly, only with the finger, not with the wrist – and he wouldn't let go. Every single note was touched, every single note! For hours! And that was just one invention! Don't ask how we worked on the Bach partitas before the recordings. Or on the Goldberg Variations. That was the most amazing thing. But I really thought, I'm done here.'

Sometimes Igor would phone Rovatkay immediately before a concert. Near the Herkulessaal in Munich there's a sheet music shop, and once Igor rang an hour and a half before the concert to say he had found music by Johann Jakob Schütz and couldn't decide which to buy. Rovatkay was uneasy about giving Igor advice so soon before a recital of Liszt and Beethoven.

But it wasn't just phrasing that Igor had learned from Rovatkay. He'd also learned intransigence.

\#

In the spring of 2004 Igor entered the Maria Callas Competition in Athens, played seven piano concertos and came joint second with a Finnish colleague, Henri Sigfridsson, twice his age, a student of Pavel Gililov (the name will be important later). A good thing, a beautiful and unexpected success. Igor was no less anxious, but he gained in confidence.

A few weeks later Igor played to the great Grigory Sokolov.

The contact was made through Sokolov's agent. Igor travelled with his mother to see him in Amsterdam, where Sokolov had a residency at the time. Kämmerling knew nothing of it. Sokolov booked Igor into a rehearsal room in the Concertgebouw.

If the appointment went well, if Sokolov liked his playing and saw potential, it could be Igor's breakthrough.

Sokolov didn't like Igor's playing.

'I was feeling quite pleased with myself – after all, I'd just won second prize in Athens. And then I play the first movement of the Schumann Fantasie and the first movement of Beethoven Sonata Opus 2 No. 2. I play, Sokolov listens, my mother is sitting in the corner at the back, and I think my playing's been absolute rubbish. He says: one positive and one negative thing that I'd like to say to you. I say: what's the positive thing? The positive thing is: it's obvious that you really love music. And that's my positive thoughts about your playing in their entirety. And then the great Grigory Sokolov took 17-year-old me apart to such an extent that not a single blade of grass remained.

He didn't let me play another note. I remember four things he said.

'Has anyone ever told you anything about articulation? Yes, I said. Him: I don't think so. You know, you play something like legato and staccato. But in music there's legato, legatissimo, sempre legato, non legato, molto legato, staccato, spiccato, pizzicato, non staccato, sempre staccato, molto staccato, staccatissimo, pizzicatissimo – do you understand? Second question: has anyone ever told you anything about dynamics? I said, probably not. Him: That's what I think too. You play something like forte and piano. But there's forte, mezzo forte, non forte, poco forte, piu forte, fortissimo, three times fortissimo, piano, mezzopiano, non piano, rinforzando, pianissimo, crescendo, decrescendo, sempre crescendo, molto crescendo. And so on. He suggested that I learn another instrument. What about the flute? He also said things like: You should be able to do things like that at 16.'
Igor asked him if he could recommend a teacher.

Sokolov says: I don't know many, but there's Pavel Gililov.
The professor who had taught Henri Sigfridsson.

Igor thanked him and went back home with his mother. Shattered.

And then, at the summer school in Salzburg, he had a row with Karl-Heinz Kämmerling.

The other participants were working with Kämmerling on various piano concertos. As usual Igor played the orchestra parts on the second grand piano, for four or five hours at a stretch. Then at the end of the evening he played himself: the Rachmaninov Corelli Variations, the piece that Kämmerling didn't like and Igor couldn't play. Igor ran it aground.

Kämmerling lost his temper and shouted at him in front of the other participants. What was going on, did he just drink all the time, it was always the same with Russians.

Later he apologized.

But Igor was done. 'It broke something in me.'

He called Henri Sigfridson and said to him: I can't go on, this man's doing me in, I can't breathe.

Sigfridsson called Gililov, who was giving a class in Krems an der Donau, an hour and a half from Salzburg. Igor went there straight away.

'And then there's this man standing in front of me: fair hair, fantastic Italian shoes, incredibly well dressed, really tasteful, dolce vita, really impressive. He asks: What would you like to play? I say: the first movement of the Schumann Fantasie. He says: Fine. I sit there, totally terrified, and play, and eventually there's this passage with this unexpected A flat, so I play, he's standing behind me, and all of a sudden he reaches for the keyboard and plays that A flat. He caught me completely off guard, but as funny as it sounds: he also unblocked me.'

Gililov had a professorship in Cologne, and for a few years Igor secretly commuted back and forth and unofficially became Gililov's student. Igor was enrolled in Hanover, and he wasn't going to change, but equally he didn't want to be restricted by it.

Gililov showed him that playing the piano didn't consist in following the rules – or at least not only that. The essential part was freedom. Lightness.

'Those were terribly important years. Gililov just pumped oxygen into me. I owe him a lot. He radiated extreme ease and relaxation. He didn't say to me: Don't do this, don't do that, don't be like that, be like this. He said: Do you hear that? Enjoy that sound.'

Lessons with Gililov were a form of rebellion for Igor. He didn't talk to anyone about it, and paid him privately.

Gililov was the first teacher who didn't tell Igor who he had to be, but left it up to him and even encouraged him to be the person he wanted to be.

'I remember', his mother recalls, 'Igor went to Cologne with the Debussy Études. He calls me up and I ask: what was the class like? – Brilliant. – What did Gililov say? – He said it was dreadful. Igor missed criticism, good positive constructive criticism. – I asked him: What are you doing now? – I'm going to practise.'

#

Six months or so later, Igor was the youngest entrant in the Artur Rubinstein Competition in Tel Aviv, his biggest competition, only held every three years, focusing on the works with which the Polish international star pianist Artur Rubinstein enjoyed his greatest successes.

Igor won the silver medal, the special prize for chamber music, the audience prize and the special prize for the best performance of obligatory contemporary pieces.

On the jury was Matti Raekallio, professor of piano at the Sibelius Academy in Helsinki, and six months after the competition he moved to Hanover.

In May 2006 Igor went to see him and asked: Can we talk?

Raekallio remembers him. When Igor asked if he could be his student, Raekallio jumped out of his chair.

'From that moment I was allowed to be a pianist. I was allowed to play what I wanted, and the part of my life that I can remembers starts in 2006. With Matti my life began to be shaped into what it is today.'

After that, Igor went to Kämmerling. He had told no one about his plan to leave Kämmerling's class. His mother knew, but no one else did.

The two of them hadn't seen each other for a long time. We need to talk, Igor said. You want to leave my class, Kämmerling said, standing in the furthest corner of the room.

Yes, Igor said.

Kämmerling asked: Who are you going to go to?

The second worst thing that a student could do to Kämmerling was to leave his class. The worst was to go, but to stay at the University.

Go to Cologne, Kämmerling says, Pavel Gililov is there, you could study with him.

Igor said: I'm studying here, my family is here, my home is here, I will always treat you respectfully, but I'm staying in Hanover.

Then I will leave the University, Kämmerling said, and I will tell the whole world that Igor Levit made it happen.

You know what, Igor said, if that's what you want, then do it.

That conversation was the last that the pair would have for many years.

Kämmerling stayed in touch with Igor's mother; he was always very respectful, from one colleague to another. He didn't say a word to Igor.

'Two or three years later I find myself walking towards him along the *Hochschule* corridor. All that time he had never greeted me, or even looked at me. But this time he stops, holds out his hand and says: You're a good fellow. And I remember how I replied: I told you so.
Subsequently we met three times for a glass of red wine and chatted very nicely. He really didn't know what to do with me. But there was something conciliatory about it, and it did become warm and personal.'

#

'When I went to Matti Raekallio, I was completely wired – and absolutely convinced that I couldn't really play well. Yes, I'd played in a lot of competitions and always got quite far, but in one of the very dark moments Kämmerling told me I would only ever be a theatre repetiteur. And for a long time I thought I couldn't play fast pieces. I thought I didn't have the hands for them. For ages I only played very slow pieces, the Corelli Variations were out, and so was the second Prokofiev concerto, the Études were out. What was in was a single Beethoven sonata, always the same one, up and down. I was deeply worried, and because I didn't want to admit it, I outwardly became an aggressive loudmouth.'

Raekallio put the sheet music of the Transcendental Études down on the piano.

Igor said: I was once told I can't play this.
Raekallio says: Are you joking?

For the first few weeks Raekallio said almost only one thing, in numerous variations: Get started at last, you can do all this.

And Igor got started. He learned the Transcendental Études, the Busoni piano concerto, Ravel's *Gaspard de la nuit*, the Diabelli Variations and some more Beethoven sonatas. 'I was finally allowed to be a pianist', Igor says. 'I was finally allowed to play.'

Raekallio was the first teacher for whom Igor wasn't primarily a pupil but also a colleague. The lesson did not consist in one of them being right and the other one not. Raekallio's attitude was different.

I see what you're doing, I see what you want, maybe try it this way.

'Matti is a friend, a partner in crime. A power. He is a pianistic force of nature. Overflowing, with enormous curiosity, always hungry, unimaginably fast – and always clear. He's a Finn, and they tend not to mince their words, but he embodies "no bullshit" better than anybody. For me Matti is an enabler. For me Matti was a reinforcer. Matti was – at a very important age – by some distance the most important teacher in my life. I'll now say four words, and I mean them with all the depth and magnitude that I could possibly muster: Matti is my friend.'

\#

Then Matti Raekallio decided to go to New York. After he left, he and Igor stayed in touch. Igor had to switch classes.

A short time afterwards Raekallio came back to Hanover. Igor was delighted, and immediately hurled himself into a series of new projects.

And then, six months later, Raekallio went back to New York.

'I felt I'd been dumped; I took it quite personally', Igor says. 'And I told him that too.'

They sat facing one another and Igor said what he thought of Raekallio's decision, and his words were not kind. Raekallio replied: 'That's what a friendship is like.' Then they were reconciled.

Teacher and pupil finally became friends, and colleagues.

Igor regularly sent him mobile phone recordings of his pieces and asked him for advice. Raekallio sometimes gave him thorough, detailed answers, and sometimes he just said: You've got to hold the quavers for longer; it says legato in the music.

'I sometimes think', Igor says, 'that Matti is the only person around me who would understand if I said, I'm not playing any more.'

#

After Matti Raekallio's departure for New York, Igor switched classes at the University for one last time: to Bernd Goetzke, for the last run-up to the concert exam.

Goetzke had also been trained by Kämmerling, and was fundamentally different from Igor's previous professors.

There's nothing noisy or defining about his character. He's minimalist. Extremely precise and exact in his work, his teaching and his thinking.

'We got on incredibly well', Igor says. 'And there's one other difference: I was already on my way. I didn't yet know the destination, but I was already travelling.'

Goetzke and Igor had known each other for a long time. 'We'd always liked each other a lot. But two or three years before I wouldn't have understood him.'

Igor respected Goetzke.

'He's very analytical, unimaginably precise with motifs and sounds. He doesn't just work with the notes of a composition, but also with the molecules. I'm rather an impatient kind of person. But it worked.'

The lessons were very physical, but with regard to content this time, rather than craft. How do you play a note in a particular context? What does a G major triad sound like in Debussy? What is the thumb doing, what's the upper voice doing, and how do they relate to one another? It's a very grown-up form of teaching; you have to bring a lot to it. Goetzke's not about mastering pieces, but penetrating them.

'I remember we were working on Beethoven's Sonata Opus 111, and the only thing he wanted to say to me was that the motif at the beginning of the first movement moves imperceptibly through the whole sonata. He just had to draw my attention to that one thing – and all of a sudden I understood the whole piece differently. And probably I understood it for the first time.'

Igor studied with Goetzke for two days, then sat his gradu-
ating *Konzertexamen*, the concert performance part of the
exam. 'When I was finished I had the feeling: everything's
going to be ok now. I've got everything I could have dreamed
of; I've developed my language with the help of a lot of
people.

'I've had so much room and so much time. No one has got
on my nerves, I haven't taken an interest in the whole world
of careers, I was able to learn my own language, hidden away
behind the walls of the University – for as long as I could.
The door outside opened at exactly the right moment, and I
stepped confidently outside. I owe all those people an eternal
debt of gratitude.

'The only thing still missing was playing.'

#

His final performance exam in May 2010 was more than a
graduation test for Igor. 'I wanted to put together a programme
that said quite clearly: this isn't just a *Konzertexamen*; this is
me. That was important to me. That was basically my big
piano recital debut in Hanover, even though strictly speaking
I had given piano recitals in Hanover before. I turned the
whole thing into less of an exam and more my statement
concert.'

The programme: Beethoven's Diabelli Variations; Wolfgang
Rihm's song cycle *Rot*, along with his friend and fellow student,
the tenor Simon Bode; then something by Schubert; and as an
encore: 'Für Elise'.

A song cycle in a *Konzertexamen*, and also 'Für Elise': an
unusual programme.

Igor got the best total marks in the history of the institution, he discovered immediately after the concert. Congratulations, you've passed, better than anyone else ever.

'That knocked me for six at the time', Igor says. 'It's one of the few things in my life that I'm proud of.'

\#

The director of the Heidelberg Spring Music Festival, Thorsten Schmidt, was sitting in the audience at Igor's graduation exam. He didn't know Igor. Eleonore Büning had called him after she got back from the Chinese trip and insisted that he go to Hanover. Immediately after the concert he invited Igor to his festival in Heidelberg, and the evening before Igor's concert debut in Heidelberg he offered him the directorship of the Chamber Music Academy.

An unknown pianist. On a gut feeling.

'Thorsten saw something in me that I hadn't remotely seen – and if I'm honest don't see even today', Igor says. 'But it worked. He trusted me, he let me get on with things. Today Thorsten is one of my most important advisers and friends, musically and professionally, but also far beyond that.'

For his 2011 debut Igor played the 'Études d'exécution transcendante' by Franz Liszt, and a year later Frederic Rzewski's 'The People United Will Never Be Defeated!' Rzewski travelled in, and it was the first time that he had heard Igor play. After the concert he came backstage and said: why do you stay seated for so long after the piece is finished? Don't do that! The piece is over, life goes on, stand up and disappear, don't make such a pianistic show of things. What matters is the music, not the romantic nonsense surrounding it.

'That was an experience that shaped me for life. It was like a shock, an impulse that sets a change in motion. From that day onwards I started focusing more and more. And I owe that impulse both to Thorsten and to Frederic – because that moment would never have existed without Thorsten's confidence in me.'

Later Igor risked playing the Goldberg Variations for the first time in Heidelberg. Before the concert Schmidt took him aside and said: Don't worry, you've got a safety net here.

'Heidelberg was the first time I felt safe on stage. Of course I know I've got to deliver – I always have to deliver. But with Thorsten I know: I can also stumble and fall. I'm just a person. That feeling was there from the start. And that's of fundamental importance for everything that happened next.'

In 2014 Igor said he wanted to devote the following year's Academy to Frederic Rzewski.

Once again: a largely unknown artist, this time an American Communist, whose pieces aren't exactly a guarantee of sell-out concerts. The plan worked out too.

So it's not true to say that nothing was happening in Igor's life. 'I always had good people around me', Igor says. 'People who believed in me. I just didn't always notice.'

#

During this time Igor's career was like an obstacle race. While other pianists, some of them younger than him, overtook him, Igor went on revolving around himself. He played, he made an effort, stumbled, got back up, stumbled again. Which left him all the more frustrated the clearer it became to him.

'For years I wasn't allowed to', Igor says. 'For years there were lots of pieces I wasn't allowed to play. Kämmerling told me over and over that I couldn't play them.

'I wanted to play those pieces. But for years I heard: you can't do this or that now, that's not yet ready, you can't do that one, that one doesn't suit you, and of course I believed it all, so I didn't do it.

'I was extremely unfree as a pianist. I thought I couldn't play fast pieces because someone had told me I didn't have the hands for it. And of course I believed that too – and the pieces that I practised anyway went wrong, for technical and psycho-logical reasons.

'Pictures at an Exhibition by Modest Mussorgsky: didn't work. Rachmaninov's Corelli Variations: a traumatic experience. The twelve Études Opus 8 by Scriabin: a disaster.

'With all due respect, they aren't the hardest pieces in the world. I failed at all of them. And I failed for me too, not only because someone else said I had failed.

'Then came the Rubinstein Competition, and I saw what I could do. No one took an interest in me, but I met a lot of fantastic people and learned to trust myself a bit more.

'Shortly after that I played to Sokolov, and he told me I couldn't do a thing – and the whole thing fell apart. And then I started to assemble the puzzle again from the beginning.

'Then came the performance for Barenboim – and down it all crashed again.

'And so it went on – there have been some total car crashes in my life, but I learned from them. I just start over again. If there's something I can't do, it doesn't bother me. I'm glad to have found something new, and I just start working.

'I never say: Shit, I've taken a fall. Only: I want to get even higher.'

#

The performance for Daniel Barenboim happened in December 2011. Maren Borchers organized the meeting. She knew the family well – her agency worked for the pianist Elena Bashkirova, Barenboim's wife, and their son Michael. The situation was the same as it had been with Sokolov: if Barenboim promoted Igor, invited him to play from time to time, perhaps took him along as a soloist on a concert tour, a lot of doors would open automatically.

Barenboim didn't have much time, because he was conducting *Don Giovanni* at La Scala Milan. Igor flew to see him and played on a grand piano in the opera house: some of the Diabelli Variations and part of Bach's Chaconne.

It didn't actually go badly.
But it didn't go well either.

'My mind was elsewhere', Igor says. 'I was madly in love with someone at the time.'

Barenboim quickly interrupted him. Looked at him. And then became very categorical.

'He said to me in a very kind way that I should think a bit more. Now that sounds kindly meant, but it was rock-hard at the time. Literally he said: "I don't need to tell you that you can play the piano well. What you can do from your gut is all well and good. But it's all unconscious. You need to become an adult." He was incredibly nice and accommodating. He said to me in a long lecture that was really important, using a lot of examples: Grow up. And he was right.'

In the Chaconne there are several long sections with a big crescendo, where the music starts quietly and gets louder and louder.

'He said to me at the time that I should plan the crescendo better. I couldn't simply say, fine, I'll just do it, as my gut told me. I had to know exactly what level I was starting on, how I wanted to climb and where I wanted to get to. Then later on, once I've completely internalized it, it sounds quite natural – then I don't ask myself those questions. But in the working process I need to know precisely what I'm doing.'

Igor was deeply unsettled. Barenboim had, albeit tacitly, been a model for many years. After the performance he broke off contact again. Even though they both live in Berlin and work in the same field, there's been no meeting, no conversation for nine years.

'I've rarely put it into words, but the fact of not having anything to do with him for years rankled deeply. I would have loved it, but we simply didn't have anything to do with each other.'

It wasn't until 2019 that they met up again. 'I think he was surprised at who was sitting in front of him. He said only: Oh, what happened to you?'

#

Café Einstein Unter den Linden and the Berlin studio of the ZDF television channel are in the same building, with the entrance to the studio around the other side. But Igor fancies an apple. There's no fruit in the Einstein and the Lafayette supermarket on Friedrichstrasse is too far away. So we walk to the Biomarkt in Friedrichstrasse station, Igor buys apples and satsumas and sticks them in his anorak pocket, then we walk back to the studio.

The *Morgenmagazin* programme is recorded here every day, the Maybrit Illner talk show every Thursday, and on Friday the culture magazine *Aspekte*, sometimes – like today – with an audience.

We're far too early.

The broadcast is a special edition for Ludwig van Beethoven's 250th birthday. The young presenter Jo Schück is moderating, and guiding us through the evening along with Igor.

A greeter who introduces herself as Charlotte channels us through the barrier and brings us into a conference room on the first floor that's being used as a dressing room today.

Igor doesn't feel like it.
He really doesn't.

He's doing it because his record company asked him to, and because Maren Borchers also asked him to, and he's doing it a bit for the sake of Jo Schück. And of course: 45 minutes of classical music on the ZDF prime-time show, on Friday evening. The broadcast gets a bit more than a million viewers – for a lot of reasons it would be very foolish to pass up the opportunity.

Igor is professional enough not to let his reluctance show.
But in fact there's one thing he wants above all: to get the show over with. In the dressing room he slumps on a chair and

fiddles around with his phone, trying to find a recording of the E flat piano sonata by Paul Dukas.

He already knows what questions are going to come.
What makes Beethoven's music so special?
What's political about Beethoven?
And what's the connection between him, Igor, the music and activism on Twitter?
As always.

Of course he's been invited here today because it's impossible to imagine a better, more famous and more high-profile guest for a Beethoven special.
From Igor's point of view, however, he's only here because Beethoven himself can't make it.

On the conference table there's a bowl of grapes, apples, bananas and satsumas. We could have saved ourselves the trip to the Biomarkt.

The director drops in for a moment, an enthusiastic man with an ironic moustache and checked trousers that are very fashionably too short, and tells us the production team's idea: rather than the usual introductory music, Igor should give a live rendition of the opening to the Waldstein Sonata, while we are shown pictures of him walking the empty studio and a bust of Beethoven speeding through Berlin at night. The sequence with the bust has already been filmed, but could Igor please quickly play through the Waldstein Sonata so that everything can be edited together perfectly in time. Igor nods.

Then in comes Jo Schück, the presenter, in buoyant mood, blue suit, white shirt.

'What are you wearing this evening, Igor?'

'Black T-shirt, these trousers, black jacket.'

'I just want to make sure we're not both walking about in blue and white. You're just playing in black now, right?'

'Makes life easier.'

Charlotte, the greeter, informs Igor that a taxi has been booked for him for after the programme.

'Tell me, have you got WLAN in here?'

'Ah, unfortunately it doesn't work in here. But you can pick it up in the foyer; I'll get you the password.'

'No, if it only works in the foyer I don't need it.'

Igor points to the fruit bowl. 'These have all been washed, yes?'

'Yes, apart from the bananas.'

Outside in the corridor someone laughs.

Igor takes a very deep breath. And exhales very deeply.

Jo Schück leaves the room, and by now Igor has found the Dukas sonata; the first few bars tinkle out of his phone, no one speaks for a few seconds and Igor stares into space.

The door opens and the make-up girl pokes her head into the room. 'My mother's coming specially today because of you. Because she's such a fan.' – 'Oh thanks, I'm glad, give her my best!'

Another few bars of Dukas.

Then Kai-Uwe Diaz Philipp comes into the room (he looks after Igor's PR at Sony International) and he slumps on a chair as well.

'Want a satsuma?' Igor asks, and takes the fruit out of his anorak. 'Catch? Here, you can eat them all.'

'Is there something wrong with them which is why you're not eating them?'

'No, but I've already had three. As if I'd offer you mouldy satsumas. The thought!'

Then he has to go downstairs. The studio is bathed in warm, golden light, the style: cosiness and bare brick. On the podium in the corner, on a Persian carpet, a grand piano.

The blocking rehearsal starts in a minute but first, please, quickly: the Waldstein Sonata. Only the first few bars, the main theme and the run, to the G major passage before the repetition, as playback for the introductory sequence. 'Sure, only the hard part, as usual', Igor says.

He concentrates, plays, mucks up the run.

'Again, please!'

Concentration again. Theme, run, premature ending at the same spot.

'I resign', Igor shouts.

'No', the director calls over the intercom into the studio, 'you have to wait till I tell you you're fired.'

Laughter.

The third time the passage works the way it's supposed to.

'Could you play it for us again? So that we have a few cut-ins.'

Then comes the blocking rehearsal, a photograph for the internet and it's still not over.

'It's all completely absurd', Jo Schück, standing on the edge, says quietly to himself. 'Our job here, all of this and, generally speaking, the fact that a person can play the Waldstein Sonata like that. Completely absurd!'

There are monitors in the foyer, showing the previous evening's Maybrit Illner talk show, on the subject of the election of the governor of Thuringia.

Oh yes, there was that too.

Jo Schück comes with us back to the dressing room, to get a video of Igor being made up on his phone.

Igor takes his phone out of his pocket. 'Do you know this piece. Have a listen, just the first two minutes. Just the first two minutes! It's fantastic! Again Paul Dukas rattles out of the speaker, the door opens, Maren Borchers comes in and takes a correspondence folder out of her bag. In it are an invitation to the *Spiegel* Berlin office party and an invitation to the Matthaie-Mahl – a famous and ancient dinner for dignitaries – in Hamburg, with a seal on the envelope. 'I want a seal like that too!' Igor exclaims.

Then there's a letter from the President's office – the President is congratulating Igor on the International Beethoven Prize and the award from the Auschwitz Committee.

'I should like to combine my greetings to you with a sign of solidarity given the noisy and aggressive hostility to which you have been exposed for some considerable time. I am appalled that you, like many others at this time, should be the target of hatred and denigration. These are attacks on the coexistence of all of us. Attacks on our democratic and liberal order, which we must all resist. I thank you very much for your commitment and courage. The important thing is that the majority must also understand: this country will not be the same if law and human dignity are attacked and threatened. The number of those who – like you – audibly and visibly stand up against anti-Semitism and racism, who fight it where they live, learn, work and are able to achieve things, must become greater.'

The letter is two pages long.
Maren Borchers: 'I think that's really touching.'
Igor: 'What?'
'That he writes to you – and what he writes. Really. I'm easily impressed by stuff like that.'
Igor, who is changing in the other corner of the room: 'Who sent the letter? The President or what? I'll write to him.'

Schück, who has been standing nearby in silence the whole time: 'We can never quite shake off that German subservience to authority, can we? We're delighted when we get a letter from the President.'
Igor: 'I'm glad that someone apart from me puts *subservience to authority* and *German* in the same sentence. I do that all the time and nobody knows what I'm talking about. Right, I'm going to open some more letters.

The programme goes exactly as Igor expected it to.

In the introduction all the big guns are on display. 'It's a global star's birthday. We're celebrating 250 years of Beethoven. One of the most important composers of all time. A citizen of the world, a visionary, a humanist. The script, delivered by Jo Schück, perfectly matches the bars from the Waldstein Sonata played by Igor, while in the film the bust of Beethoven dashes through Berlin. Jo Schück carries on, while Igor continues playing. 'Now the special broadcast in the jubilee year of this exceptional talent, with an exceptional talent from the present day. He is one of the best pianists in the world. And he has also been given awards for his social commitment, amongst others the International Beethoven Prize. Ladies and Gentlemen: Igor Levit.'

The last notes are drowned by the applause of the studio audience. Igor and Jo Schück take their seats on a brown leather sofa, with Beethoven's signature projected on a screen behind them like an autograph. In front of the camera Schück becomes more formal.

'We are talking about a man who would just have turned 250, who has shaped the whole world with his music. Even you, Herr Levit, have said you have your happiest moments with Beethoven. Why is that?'

Igor looks tired and thinks for a moment.
He could say any old thing, he could give an old answer, what is known in the trade as: speaking on autopilot.

But autopilot is too boring for Igor.

So, a new answer: 'It's simply because that music has not only accompanied me since my earliest childhood, but has also given me a kind of safe zone. For lots of reasons. I'm a human being, I always need the unknown. If I see a door over there and don't know what's behind the door, I have to go through it. I'm always looking for new things. And that curiosity, novelty, constant risk, danger, is something that shapes that music to an unusual extent. And it just inspires me from day to day. It's always new, always new, and it always keeps you awake. And in that danger, in that unknown, I just feel safe.'

Igor has packed a lot of loose ends into that answer – it's a bit too complex for the format, and would need a lot of secondary questions – but Schück has to move on to the next subject. And also they're about to show the first clip: the team did a vox pop, showing people in the street in night-time Berlin a bust of Beethoven and asking them to guess who it is. Goethe? Schiller?

Immediately after that, the next question to Igor. Any tips for first-time listeners? Questions like that don't get you far with Igor. 'I would', he says, 'recommend everything.'

Then they sit him down at the piano, to explain what is special about Beethoven's music.
Ok.
Igor cites the example of the Moonlight Sonata. 'First of all, Beethoven uses the music to open up a space that a person then enters.' He plays the first few bars of the Moonlight

Sonata, the slow triplets, and a deep calm immediately settles over the studio. Then the G flat in the right hand, the voice calling into the space. The audience members in the front few rows smile knowingly.

Then Igor shows a phrase from the fugue in the Hammerklavier Sonata and the conclusion of the Appassionata, two little moments of high-wire artistry, in which Igor just manages not to fall into the net. Here too, in front of a million-strong audience, expression remains important. Not all the notes are in exactly the right place, but he knows the audience is aware: in a concert he could do it. And that's what matters. The fact that more people are listening than ever would be in a concert – too bad.

After a clip on the history of the reception of the 9th Symphony and its appropriation by a great variety of regimes and ideologies – there is a famous recording of a concert with Wilhelm Furtwängler for Hitler's birthday, and no less famous is the performance at the G20 summit in Hamburg – Jo Schück turns to the question of Igor as a political artist.

'How are your art and your political life connected? Do artists have a different kind of responsibility from normal citizens?' – 'I don't know. I don't connect my music-making with my political activism; there's nothing to connect. It's my life, they are the two most important pillars in my life. I'm not going to stop loving music. And I'm not going to stop being active and an activist.'

Schück reads a two-day-old tweet from Igor on the crisis in Thuringia. '75 years after the liberation of Auschwitz, in 2020 German politics is legitimizing Björn Höcke and his gang of fascists. This isn't going to be some edifying now-more-than-ever tweet. There is nothing edifying. I could weep.' Igor tapped out the text during the recordings of the Stevenson Passacaglia.

'Nothing has changed', Igor says. 'It was a total political shock. I mean, for years that gang has been normalized, sometimes by the media, sometimes politically, in spite of all kinds of warnings. Two days ago the party was elevated to the status of king-maker. And even if we go on to have new elections in Thuringia: the genie is out of the bottle, the dam has broken. And the failure of political conservatives in this country, I continue to stand by this, will do us very great harm in the future.'

The audience applauds.

What, Schück wants to know in conclusion, would he say to those people who tell him he should stick to playing the piano and not constantly express his political opinions?

'That bores me', Igor says. 'That kind of statement. "Shut up and play", that bores me, and those people, the members of this civil society, who threaten politicians and mostly women, quite honestly, pardon my language: to hell with them. I don't spend a second longer on that than I need to.'

75 years after the liberation of Auschwitz.
Björn Höcke and his gang of fascists.
Normalized by the media and politics.
To hell with them.

There's nothing wrong with these words, on the contrary.
They would not be remarkable if more people found the courage to utter them rather than believing them in silence.
But because only a few find the courage to do it on a prime-time ZDF programme in front of a million viewers, it is remarkable.

Not because of Igor or because of the words.
But because the person who says them is such a lone voice.

The political segment is exactly four minutes long.

Then Jo Schück moves on to the next clip: *Fidelio*, Beethoven's only opera. Later Igor has to guess some quotations and also play a bit more piano: the Moonlight Sonata again, and 'Für Elise'.

And then it's done. At last.
They moved on easily.

'That went ok, didn't it?' Igor asks Jo Schück and the director in the lift on the way to the production rooms where – as always after a recording – a swift glass is raised to the programme. The director first calls in at the cutting room, because he has to shorten the programme before it's broadcast to fit the channel's schedules. 'We ran on a bit too long', the director says. 'But really barely at all.' – Schück: 'Well, six or seven minutes isn't that great.' – It's only four', the director says. 'We'll manage.'

And which four minutes might that be?

Over drinks in the *Aspekte* production room, Igor talks about his appearance on the Maybrit Illner show, and the conversation that *BILD*'s Berlin office chief Ralf Schuler, who talked to him about his tweet during the programme, wanted to have with him afterwards.

'You know what he did after the programme? First stir things during the programme. And then afterwards we're standing there in the lobby, he comes up to me and says, Herr Levit, another thing I wanted to say to you, I make music too, I play drums! Haha! Yes exactly.'

Igor's taxi is waiting. He says goodbye and takes the lift down with Maren Borchers.

'I don't want them to cut out me saying "To hell with Nazis!"' – 'They will, though.' – 'But that's horrible.' – 'No, it's the right thing to do.' – 'Maybe you're horrible.' – 'Can we talk for a moment?' – 'No, I want to go home.'

Igor gets wearily into the taxi, while Maren Borchers and Kai-Uwe Daiz Philipp, the record company's PR man, stand next to the door and analyse his appearance. Maren Borchers calls after Igor: Have a nice evening!

'What do you think?' – 'Well, it was fine, I can't see many weaknesses in it. It always gets very personal very quickly, I'm not sure if that's always such a good thing. But he gave good answers.' – 'Sometimes I'd like a more clearly formulated message.' – 'Even more clearly?' – 'But I thought the politics bit was exactly right, and that, I agree with you, was something completely different. It went off in all directions at the same time. Shame they're cutting it out.'

Two hours later the programme is broadcast on ZDF. The piano passages sound rounder and fuller than they did in the studio, the dialogue is faster, with fewer pauses for thought.

The four minutes of politics are untouched.

#

Hamburg, 10 March 2020. On the day of his thirty-third birthday, Igor gives a concert in the Elbphilharmonie in Hamburg: Beethoven's Piano Concertos No. 3 and No. 5 as soloist with the Kammerakademie Potsdam under the conductor Antonello Manacorda.

The evening before, he tweets a photograph from the Grand Hall of the Elbphilharmonie, along with the line: 'Where I'm allowed to celebrate my thirty-third.' The hall is empty, with a concert grand on the stage.

At the weekend German health minister Jens Spahn has advised a prohibition on events with over 1,000 participants.

The audience is very slightly sparser than usual. A repeat of the concert is planned for the following day in Hanover, and a few days after that Igor is due to play Liszt's Piano Concerto No. 1. The date now looks very uncertain. No one saw this coming. And if they did, they tried not to believe it.

When Igor steps onto the stage of the Elbphilharmonie in the evening, a man calls down from the balcony: 'Happy Birthday!' Igor blows him a kiss.

The moderator is the man who came up ten years ago with the idea of Igor recording the Beethoven sonatas: Michael Becker, artistic director of the Tonhalle Düsseldorf.

'We've known each other for quite a long time', Becker says to Igor and the audience, 'and since mobile phones have existed you've had one. And it's very noticeable that you write a very great deal, that you express opinions about lots of things and that you're hardly ever off the stage. Do you become someone else on stage? Or is it the same person, who's able to switch so quickly?'

'I've never wanted to switch. That's never been a thing for me. For me going on stage and making music is basically a natural continuation of my life, my day. I don't act out roles. I've never acted out roles. I look forward to being on stage when I'm backstage just as much as I look forward to the rest of the day when I'm on stage. It's just my life that's happening here.'

Piano Concerto No. 3 is the only Beethoven piano concerto that's in a minor key. The piano concerto has an extended orchestral exposition, a hundred bars, about three and a half minutes of music before the soloist comes in – that was the convention, the ensemble prepares for the soloist's entry and establishes the themes that he then picks up, varies and extends, plays off against each other, while at the same time defending them.

Piano Concerto No. 5, on the other hand, starts with a bang for the soloist. 'I think it's one of the piano concertos that are often misunderstood', Igor says. 'It's one of the most chamber-music-style, the most elegant concertos that I know; the piano is often the instrument accompanying the orchestra rather than the other way round. And it's a profoundly dignified, human piece, with a second movement that goes straight to the heart. It's a wonderful piece of music that deserves something better than the nickname "Emperor".'

Igor is almost bursting with energy and anticipation. He can hardly sit still on the piano stool, bouncing up and down, playing apparently effortlessly. Everything's right, everything works. He is in the very best of form.
After the concert, then, backstage: big birthday wishes, a lot of Igor's friends were at the concert and are now backstage in the queue for the cloakroom. Igor is cheerful and happy.
But not entirely.

What's up?
'I don't know', Igor says.
What was it like out there?

'Strange. Have you read *The Radetzky March*, by Joseph Roth? It felt like that. You have a sense of something coming to an end.'

In the Elbphilharmonie the audience and artists need to have left the building within an hour of the end of the concert or the organizers get slapped with a supplement to the rent of the hall. In the restaurant opposite, the concert organizer has put on a birthday dinner, everything is ready, but no one really wants to leave.

Text from Igor the next day at 11.43.
'Sad, tell you later.'
'Are you playing in Hanover?'
'No.'
'Merkel and Spahn are speaking at the government press conference. They're talking about an epidemic that might last for months, maybe years.'
'But they're not thinking of closing everything down for months and years?'
'Doesn't look that way.'
'Ok. So?'
'They don't know.'
'And that's the worst thing.'

The sentence from *The Radetzky Match* that Igor was referring to was:
He saw a world collapsing, and it was his world.

#

The day after the concert in the Elbphilharmonie, Igor was due to play the same programme again with the Kammerakademie Potsdam in Hanover. From there he was supposed to travel to Cologne to talk about James Baldwin with the author Carolin

Emcke and the actor Jerry Hoffmann at the LitCologne literary festival. Both dates were cancelled, as was everything else.

Instead, Igor travelled from Hamburg to Berlin, to the place in the world that he knows least: home.

'I walked from the supermarket to my place with two shopping bags in my hand and thought about the question I'd had in my head since the concert in the Elbphilharmonie: what am I going to do now? I wasn't clear how long the period without concerts would go on for – but it was immediately clear to me that it would last longer than just one or two weeks. And then I thought: right, I'm going to get through this period.'

At 14.42 he writes on Twitter.

'The concert halls are empty, and listening to and experiencing music is not possible. That's sad, but it's necessary. And it's fine that way. None the less I would like to go on sharing music with you. Listening, experiencing. As best I can. So I'm trying something out: my concert from home. The audience is all of you. From this evening at 7.00 pm, I'm going to play for you from my home. Via livestream, here on Twitter. What's on the programme? I don't know yet. I'll have a look. It's an experiment. Social media concert from home. Until we can all get together, in real life, side by side, and experience art again. So, tonight at 7.00. I look forward to seeing you. Igor.'

'I often do that', Igor says. 'I throw an idea into the air, and only then do I see what it does with me, how it develops and what its consequences are.'

The tweet immediately goes viral.

There are four hours till the start of the concert that he's announced.

He meets up with Georg Diez, who is nearby at a Japanese bakery, and tells him about his idea. Diez at first misunderstands him, and thinks he wants to stream out of empty concert halls.
'No, from my living room', Igor says.
'Oh. Wow. Go ahead', Diez says.
He grasps the extent of the idea even before Igor has done so himself.

An artist contacting his audience directly, without the machinery of the classical music business – no organizer and no concert hall, no ticket sales or programme discussions, and no media to direct people's attention. Of course, for now it's only a streamed concert, but if you think the thing through, a concert broadcast from home assumes an almost revolutionary momentum: the power to decide what happens and what doesn't is back in the artist's hands. The hands of the player who might otherwise be the focus of the concert business, but has little to say in the end.

Because it is always other people who determine who can play what for whom, and what for. Not a problem for established artists in a good negotiating position. But for most of his life Igor was an unestablished artist, who saw himself exposed to the whims of the market, and even today he can't break away from that.

This afternoon there's another aspect that's much closer to his heart.

'I knew I wouldn't manage to make music just for myself. There are psychological reasons for that, reasons to do with emotional self-preservation. I needed music to survive those days. But I also needed a reason to sit down at the piano.'

However, he has no idea how to do it: stream a concert.

Igor cycles to the electrical shop on Alexanderplatz and buys a stand for his phone for 25 euros. Cycles home again. Then cycles back because he's realized that he needs a bracket to hold the phone on the stand.

On the way he calls his friend the journalist Melissa Chan in California to solve another significant fundamental problem: is it technically possible to put a stream up on Twitter that's longer than a few minutes? Chan asks someone who works at Twitter and calls Igor back a few minutes later. Yes, it's not a problem.

At 7 in the evening Igor sits down in his socks at the grand piano and plays the Waldstein Sonata, with about 80,000 people listening live. In all, more than 300,000 watched the recording.

The sound quality is modest, and the programme automatically lowers the volume on the louder passages. The piano sounds as if the sound engineer were just holding a phone rather than a microphone up to the artist during a recording – and that's exactly what's happening, except without the sound engineer. Igor's phone had also fallen into the margarine over breakfast in Hamburg.

But this moment has a quite different quality. Via the comments function listeners are aware of the presence of the others. Even though most of them are sitting by their smartphone screens in the living room at home, a potent sense of community emerges.

At first Igor doesn't notice. 'I spent 20 minutes praying inwardly that Twitter wouldn't interrupt the transmission.'

After the concert he decided that from now on he would actually play every evening.

#

Then there was supposed to be a concert after all. In Munich, on the stage of the National Theatre, with the Bavarian State Orchestra under the conductor Joana Mallwitz. She and Igor have known each other since the Early Promotion programme of the *Hochschule* in Hanover. As children they entered countless competitions together, ate gummy bears and told jokes backstage, and both are now global superstars.

Given that the theatres and opera houses in Bavaria had remained closed for ages because of the Covid situation, the concert was to take place without an audience, and would be streamed on the Opera House website.

On the programme: Franz Schubert's Unfinished and Franz Liszt's Piano Concerto No. 1, with Igor as soloist.

Igor turns up and the two of them practise. It's an important date for Mallwitz. In the summer she was due to conduct at the Salzburg Festival, the first woman ever, and the country's most notable music journalists had insisted on being unofficially smuggled into the viewing room for the big advance profiles in the papers.

But nothing came of it.

Early in the morning on the day before the concert the date was unexpectedly cancelled, because there was a suspected Covid case in the orchestra. Instead, several small ensembles were to play a replacement programme that would be transmitted on the internet that evening. So that Igor didn't have to set off straight away, his manager agreed on a solo performance by Igor: alone on the stage of the empty National Theatre, he would play the Diabelli Variations.

The light was dimmed, and he played into the void, into the blackness of the auditorium. In the box to the side, out of range of the cameras, was his manager. There was no one else in the audience.

'There we all were right in the middle of *The Radetzky March*', Igor would say a few days later. 'You could basically hear the cannon in the distance, and you knew: it's over. As on the last three pages of Mahler's Ninth – it's clear, it's over, very quiet and still.'

What did the empty auditorium feel like from the stage?

'It was ok. I really like that auditorium. But it was also ok because the auditorium wasn't in fact completely empty. You just saw me. I had Kristin sitting here in front of me, and that's enough for me. In the end this concert was just one more illusion. One last twitch. Afterwards I just said, bye, Kristin, we won't see each other again for a bit. And that's what happened. Then I went to the airport, the terminal was almost empty. And from the next day it was all over.'

#

A day in March or April, it doesn't matter which. Igor is sitting at home and, because he can't meet anyone or go anywhere, travelling into his own musical past.

'I'm listening again to records that I constantly listened to as a student, the whole time, non-stop. I'm listening to them again now, and I still think they're incredibly brilliant.

Dr Dre, Snoop Dogg, Eminem, most of all Eminem.

'They put you in such a good mood, they're sensationally well made, I go completely nuts every time I hear them. It's music that made a big impression on me. I keep asking myself: Why did they do it like that? And then I listen again, again and again, and then I know why.'

The music spoke to him in a phase of his life when he didn't know where he was headed. Until then he had played an awful lot of piano and done relatively little else in his life; he felt too fat and ignored, and compensated for his self-doubt with too much ego. He was having problems in school and struggling to find his way into the life that thirteen-, fourteen- and fifteen-year-olds led in Hanover around the millennium.

A teenager, musically very gifted, but more despairing than cheerful about it. Anxious, with too much talent and mischief to find a normal-tempered everyday life interesting and, as a result of years of preoccupation with music, with too much emotion and too much sensibility to know what to do with himself.

'And then this young rapper comes along, who calls himself Eminem, and whose message essentially consists of one word: I. Every single album that he recorded in the first ten years is one big autobiography. I thought it was incredibly brave and brilliant that somebody would build his whole journey on the word "I" – and not give a damn about what "one" does and doesn't do. Eminem caught me right in the middle of a time when I'd worked out for myself: "I want to be able to say 'I'."'

Igor was first in line outside the record shop in Hanover when a new album came out, and then he would listen to the record uninterrupted for days.

Years later he would say in an interview that he'd learned more about Beethoven from Eminem than he had from Beethoven. When you listen to Igor playing, that seems understandable; in the insistence on individual statements, in the perfection in it that's supposed to come across like improvisation, in the unqualified determination to make oneself the subject.

'That's so good! So well written! Those lyrics and that rhythm! Then I listen to it thoroughly and analyse the tracks one by one: this word is faster than that one and slower than this one – I really listen my way into it. It's part of my DNA. Without question! Except unfortunately Eminem's music sounds awful on the piano.'

#

Matti Raekallio drew Igor's attention to Ferruccio Busoni. 'Busoni is Matti's hero', Igor says. 'He did his doctorate on Busoni's fingering. And then he brought Busoni closer to me, and then he became my hero too.'

A man with a full, mild face, a cool gaze and the mane of a maestro, who was one of the greatest pianists of his day in the earliest years of the last century. Busoni was a virtuoso pianist, composer and conductor, not only of the classics but also of contemporary music – but the contemporary music of his own time: born in 1866 in Empoli, 30 kilometres south of Florence, died in Berlin in 1924. He lived his earliest years as a prodigy; the next as a virtuoso, composer and teacher; the last as a visionary. Busoni studied in Vienna; taught in Leipzig, Helsinki, Moscow and Boston; finally moved to Berlin at 28 and spent the years around the First World War in exile in Zurich. He was a contemporary of Gustav Mahler and Richard Strauss, beside whom his music sounds almost modest and undramatic.

He composed pieces that are really too big for the piano. An eighty-minute concerto for piano, orchestra and male voice choir, for example. Or the *Fantasia Contrappuntistica* – an attempt to complete the final part of Johann Sebastian Bach's *Art of the Fugue*. As well as this, there are various treatments and transcriptions of organ works by Johann Sebastian Bach for piano, including ten chorale preludes. Some of these now sound as if they were the work of American jazz pianists.

He looked at Bach's works with the techniques of late Romanticism, produced a complete edition of Bach for the music publishers Breitkopf & Härtel and authored a fifty-four-page essay that the music critic Hans Heinz Stuckenschmidt called 'a piece of the true utopia'. 'No one could have expressed the call for new orders more clearly, more imaginatively or more poetically.' A book full of optimism, unsystematic and unworkable, not a textbook and not an academic work either, but a manifesto. The title: *Sketch of a New Aesthetic of Music*.

Reading this book helps you understand Igor.

They are the notes of someone who wants to explain the world. Busoni sees music not as a venerable art form as old as day and night, whose traditions and conventions are unassailable. He considers music with a fresh eye, seeing music above all as what it could be but isn't allowed to be.

'Music as an art, so-called Western music, is barely 400 years old, it lives in a state of development; perhaps the very first stage of an as yet unpredictable development, and still we speak of classics and sanctified traditions.'

Music is floating and weightless, transparent and almost bodyless; it consists of nothing but sounding air. To be even more precise: music is free. 'Music was born free', Busoni writes, 'and to win freedom is its destiny.'

Most important to Igor is the section in which Busoni engages with sheet music. 'Notation, the writing down of pieces of music, is first and foremost an ingenious device for capturing an improvisation in order to resurrect it.'

The performer's task is to loosen up the rigidity of the signs and put them in motion, Busoni writes. 'But legislators demand that the performer reproduce the rigidity of the signs, and revere the reproduction as all the more perfect the more it keeps to the signs.' For them, the signs themselves are the most important thing. 'If it were up to the legislators, a single piece of music would always be played in the very same tempo, however often, by whom and under whichever conditions it was played. But it is not possible, the floating expansive nature of the divine child resists; it demands the opposite. Each day begins differently from the one before, and yet always with a sunrise.'

Great artists repeatedly play their own works differently, 'they recraft them in a moment, they speed them up and hold back – as they could not record in signs – and always according to the given conditions of that eternal harmony.' One of the key sentences: 'What the composer inevitably forfeits in terms of his inspiration through these signs, the performer should restore with his own.'

That has consequences for every concert.

'The creator should accept no traditional law in blind faith,' Busoni writes. 'The creator's task lies in establishing his own laws rather than following them. Anyone who follows given laws ceases to be a creator.'

So playing a Beethoven sonata does not mean following all the instructions – placing each tone in the place where the sheet music says it should be, with the exact prescribed intensity, and relying on all the correctly placed notes producing the sonata. Instead, music should be understood as a means of expression, in the best sense: as language with which a whole world can be narrated, a truth that lies behind the notes – and which can be different from one time to the next, or which must even, strictly speaking, be different in order to avoid falling into a routine.

'Routine transforms the temple of art into a factory,' Busoni writes. 'It destroys creativity. Because creativity means: creating out of nothing. One would like to cry out: avoid routine, begin each time as if you had never begun, know nothing, but think and feel!'

That is the essence for me, Igor says. 'The utopian idea of total freedom. As unattainable as it is, so important it is to me.'

So when Igor sits down at the piano and plays the Hammerklavier Sonata: do we hear the sound of Beethoven or Igor? 'Beethoven, of course,' Igor says, 'but played by me.'

#

Apart from Eminem and Busoni, Igor has a third musical idol who has – starting in his teenage years – left a lasting mark on him: the jazz pianist Thelonious Monk.

'In the twentieth century, Thelonious Monk is probably my greatest hero alongside Ferruccio Busoni. For me Monk is freedom made reality, he is one of the most significant composers of the twentieth century. The tone is already there in him, without preamble, without flourishes, quite simple but filled with strength. As unwieldy as the music is, as angular and even cramped as it is – for me there's no one who can touch him.

There's a scene in *Blood Sport*, an incredibly bad film, in which Jean-Claude van Damme has to break a stack of cement blocks. And then someone says to him: you're only allowed to break the one at the bottom, all the others have to be left whole. And he doesn't take a swing, he just exerts pressure, and sure enough, only the one on the bottom breaks. That's the kind of playing I'm talking about. Radical, fast, free and fearless.

You need to be fearless to dare to produce a note without a long run-up. You need to have incredible confidence, in yourself, in your nerves, and in your body. That's what Monk represents for me: freedom, fearlessness, speed, depth, pain.

He said one very famous thing that was a very great support to me when I understood it: the piano ain't got no wrong notes. In other words, there are only your notes.

Of course that doesn't mean that I can always play G flat instead of F flat; that would be idiotic.

But it means that there's basically no wrong way of playing a piece because conversely there isn't only one correct way.

However I play a piece – it has its justification, because it's my way. Of course no one is obliged to like the result, but no one can say it's wrong. It has its claim to validity.

'Because without me as a performer the music would not exist at all at that moment.

The way Monk speaks, the way he plays, and the way he sits at the piano and doesn't care whether a note is beautiful or not, as long as it is simply there, because it is his note in any case – that way of doing things has always fascinated me.

As a student I thought Monk was a much more significant, perhaps not a better, but certainly a greater composer than Arnold Schoenberg. As far as I'm concerned, he's on that level, no question.

I always wanted to be like Monk. He's my hero. A pole star.

For me, *the piano ain't got no wrong notes* means: have courage, Igor. Have the courage to trust in yourself. Don't make yourself smaller than you are.'

#

A career is defined by three factors: the pieces you play. The places where you play them. And collaboration with certain other musicians.

A lot of careers are asserted and overdetermined with big stories, and the same is true of Igor's career, his former fellow student Simon Bode says. 'When you look at the biography it's as if he just walked through it; everything was effortless and speedy and fast. If you take a closer look at his journey, it really isn't the case. There are many years of dog work behind it. The reasons for Igor's success are instinct, talent and luck. He himself has told me that over and over again. It could all have turned out differently.'

Bode is one of his oldest friends. They met in 2002 at Jugend Musiziert; the competition played out on a region, state and federal level. Afterwards Igor and Simon got a grant from the Jürgen Ponto Foundation, appeared in Frankfurt in front of top bankers, and afterwards at the Schlosstheater in Schwetzingen. Simon's professor and Kämmerling knew each other from Hanover. Simon started out as a law student but then switched to the *Hochschule* and studied singing, and today he's in demand as a lyric tenor. He doesn't just know Igor better than most, he's also known him for longer.

'Igor always had this tone that meant you could tell after three bars: that's Igor playing', he says. 'It's a big, generous tone, without becoming wobbly and rotund. Incredibly precise and bright in attack, but without being harsh. It never produces a thing in order to display it. Nothing is asserted; what he plays is just there. A combination of generosity and precision.'

Has Igor always had the compass to know, I want that and I'm going to do it? 'He had that compass', Simon Bode says. 'But I don't know if he himself was always sure of it. That is, no: I know he wasn't.'

A career, Simon Bode says, is always the result of a struggle.

Equally crucial in many cases are things and moments whose significance is not immediately apparent, and which only pay off later. And sometimes not at all.

\#

After the Rubinstein Competition in 2005, Igor came back to Hanover and kept going as before.

'Not a soul was interested in me. I didn't make a huge name for myself in the world of concerts, I didn't go on tour, there were no famous conductors to protect me, and no agencies. It's not as if I didn't have anyone around me – there were always fantastic people who believed in me, even if I didn't at the time. But the headlines I'd hoped for didn't happen. From today's perspective, that was one of the biggest gifts in my life.'

Careers that start with winning a big competition are standard in the field. They usually follow the same pattern: learn the repertoire, record an album, go on tour for two years. Then the next programme, the next CD, the next tour.

There actually were a few concerts. Igor travelled across Israel, giving one recital after another. But no one discovered him. He stayed in his league; he played small and medium-sized festivals, not the big houses. He had time to learn some repertoire.

'From the perspective of those days, of course, I couldn't have been more excited. You're 17 or 18, you're not rich, you have no angle. You just want to make a career and be on a big agency's lists, if you're ambitious, and I was. I never got bored of that ambition, which is why I never let things get me down.'

That was because he had people around him who recognized and fed his talent. Martin Brauss, the director of the Institute for the Early Promotion of the Musically Gifted in Hanover. Frederic Rzewski, Lajos Rovatkay. 'But I sought most of it myself.'

'That was the time when he suffered', his mother says. 'And I did too, a lot. He suffered because he wasn't going forwards.

And when you don't go forwards, it's very difficult for an artist. Because there's no air.'

'Of course at the time I had one or two conversations with agents', Igor says, 'because I thought I was good at talking about myself. I just went and stood at the back.'

A better starting point than Hanover is hard to imagine. The *Hochschule* has one of the best piano departments in the world, where Karl-Heinz Kämmerling, Hans Leygraf, Bernd Goetzke have all made their contributions over the decades. 'In our class it was all top-class pianists, one after another. There were some really fantastic players.' Some of the most important music agencies are in the city.

The first discussion with an agent was a failure.

'He sat opposite me, looked at me and then asked to hear me play. We went to the University and I played him a few bars of the first Brahms piano concerto. He didn't think it was any good, he gave me advice about what to do differently, he tried to give me a lesson. And then came the question about which "big conductors" I'd played with. I said: If I'd played with a lot of big conductors, why would I need you? Then he gave me a long lecture: the agency he worked for had no time and no capacity to build careers. He didn't take me on, thank God.'

For Igor the conversation isn't the only one that ends with this question.

Who have you played with so far?
Nobody really.
Ok, thank you.

'Every one of those conversations really annoyed me. I was at a difficult age, an inexperienced 18-year-old, and everything was coming together.'

Only individual colleagues fed and encouraged him.

The pianist Hans-Christian Wille, a former student of Kämmerling's, brought him to his festival in Braunschweig and had him play.
Kari Kahl-Wolfsjäger brought him to the Bad Kissingen Summer Festival.
Gerrit Glaner of Steinway became an important colleague, adviser and friend. Martin Brauss, the founder of the Institute for the Early Promotion of the Musically Gifted in Hanover, gave him a lot of support. The Jürgen Ponto Foundation organizes concerts in the northern state of Mecklenburg-Vorpommern; the violinist Maxim Vengerov took him on tour as accompanist. It's not as if nothing was going on, just not nearly enough.

But then a collaboration with an agent did come. And collapsed again.

It's hard to say how Igor would have developed if the first conversations with agencies had been more successful. 'I would have been easier to manipulate, 100 per cent. But at some point I just said out of some inner rage: Ok, if it doesn't matter anyway, I'll just do what I want.'

#

In 2006 Igor performed his debut in the Kleiner Sendesaal in Hanover, in the 'Pro Musica' series. A big concert promoter wanted to give him a contract, and the documents were ready for signature.

Everyone was there. Everyone knew he was the next person from the *Hochschule* to make it. His programme was relatively brave: Robert Schumann's Fantasie in C major, two Mozart sonatas, KV 457 in C minor and KV 282 in E flat major, the Duport Variations and Prokofiev's Piano Sonata No. 7. Brave because the pieces demanded not so much virtuoso skill as inner maturity, and not just technical but also creative perfection. By now he was 19, and had been studying in Hanover for six years.

'I remember he ran away a bit with the Mozart sonata', Simon Bode says. 'I thought, yes, perhaps not exactly the way he rehearsed it, but it's also beautiful the way he loses himself in the moment.' It didn't match the ideal way that Mozart was supposed to sound according to the prevailing academic opinion.

'He rocks back and forth, he frowns or smiles pleasurably to himself. It looks as if a musical vision is flowing through the whole of Igor Levit's body, before settling in his fingers and discharging themselves on to the Steinway', writes the music critic of the *Hannoversche Allgemeine Zeitung* who's on duty that night. 'His playing is noticeable for its imaginative richness, its musicality, its capacity for dreamy contemplation', and Igor Levit 'came into his own particularly in quiet, dreamy and songlike moments.'

Then things became less kind.

The E flat major sonata strove for effect as if trying to say the same thing. Levit decorated all the repetitions with ornaments and lost himself in pretentiously emphasized details that halted the melodic flow and made the tempo uneven.

That's not how you play Mozart.

His interpretations were threatened 'not by smoothness, but by creative arrogance, by an unbridled obsession with detail

– the Mozart was over-emphatic, Prokofiev's piano sonata not purposeful enough. The closing sentence: 'Levit still lacks the unconditional determination to hold the audience prisoner.'

The following day Igor went to the contract signing, but there was no longer a contract. The concert organizers had withdrawn their offer. Nobody who played Mozart like that was marketable.

#

In 2007 Igor was given his first engagement on a cruise ship, as a soloist with the English Chamber Orchestra – the violinist Maxim Vengerov had found him the job. Also on board was the solo oboist François Leleux. He called him a year later because the Chamber Orchestra of Europe was planning a tour with the conductor Vladimir Jurowski, and with Richard Strauss's orchestral suite *Le bourgeois gentilhomme*. It has a piano part – did Igor want to play it? Igor agreed – and on the tour he met Hélène Grimaud, who was playing Maurice Ravel's G major piano concerto in the first part of the programme.

Igor asked her if he could play for her. Sure, she said, but where? In the Alte Oper in Frankfurt they had 20 minutes before the orchestra came on stage for rehearsal. Igor played the Diabelli Variations, and had to break off two-thirds of the way through because the first musicians were coming into the auditorium. She joined him on stage and said, 'I am mesmerised.'

'Hélène was probably the first famous musician who said to me: You're special. She said she had listened to me practising on this tour, and hoped that her impression would turn out to be right. She saw me in a way in which I hadn't even started to see myself – in a phase in my career in which nothing at all was happening.'

She asked him: Who works for you? He said: Nobody really. She asked: Do you have a record company? He said: No, but I've got an offer from a small label. She said: Are you mad? In five years you'll be right up at the top, don't sign just anything right now.

She recommended her agent, Jasper Parrott.

\#

In 2009 Igor met Jasper Parrott, the impresario and co-founder of the British agency Harrison Parrott.

Igor was travelling again, on a cruise ship with the English Chamber Orchestra.

Parrott heard him play the Diabelli Variations, watched him over a period of time, and they chatted on the cruise. A few months later he signed him up.

Their collaboration began a year before the big profile in the *Frankfurter Allgemeine Sonntagzeitung.*

But the rocket still didn't take off. Igor got more recitals, most of them better funded, so there was that. The Harrison Parrott stamp helped. But Igor didn't feel seen and understood, and the management relied on quantity. 'All at once', Igor says, 'it was a huge amount'. Rather than twenty concerts a year, Igor was soon playing about a hundred.

During that period he encountered a problem from his student days again. 'During that time I heard the pronoun "one" a lot. One must do this, one must not do that, Igor, have patience before you can take this step you first have to take another step. They had a template for how artists are built up and the course that careers should take. But the template didn't work in my case. I wasn't interested in the word "one"; I didn't want to hear people saying: Be patient! 16,000 things were going on in my head at once, and that wasn't their language.'

Igor played along for four years. He took care of the things that mattered to him all by himself, which didn't make working with the agency any easier.

He played his debut in the Brahms Hall of the Vienna Musikverein, on his own.

He became director of the Chamber Music Academy on the Heidelberg Spring Festival and no one from the agency showed up. Igor felt abandoned.

#

Igor repeatedly heard other people saying he was a good pianist, but unfortunately he was a boring, odd, unmarketable nerd. 'It wasn't that I had no contacts, but that people simply refused to talk to me.'

Igor was seen as a huge talent, but only partly taken seriously. 'An oddball who's constantly telling strange jokes, and you're never sure if he's really got it together, because he talks so much', a friend said. A huge potential with a huge ego, to mask his insecurity.

Then a notable classical label took an interest in him. At their introductory conversation they said they needed a story that would help them sell Igor as a person – he hadn't by any chance grown up poor or anything?

'I got incredibly angry. I said to them at the time, you know, if I tell you that on 4 December 1996 we were at Düsseldorf airport, that we needed a luggage trolley and for hours my parents couldn't come up with the words to change some money to get one: today that sounds like a nice little anecdote. But it wasn't, it was a dramatic moment, my parents had just given up their life! Who do you actually think you are?'

The conversation lasted no longer than necessary. After that he severed contact.

#

On a Thursday in May 2011 Igor gave a concert in the Berlin Radialsystem. This auditorium is right by the River Spree, in an old nineteenth-century pump works – steel, glass and bare brick. Igor played a little series of variation works. This time it was the Diabelli Variations, a fifty-minute concert.

In the audience was Anselm Cybinski. Until then he knew Igor only from his profile in the *Frankfurter Allgemeine Sonntagszeitung*. When the article came out, Cybinski was about to switch from being head of publicity at ECM to become executive producer at Sony. After the first few bars his scepticism made way for fascination. 'The way he sat there, the way he concentrated all the energy in the room, the way he formed sounds, related the different tempi together, the way he gave each individual variation an urgency and energetic charge – it was really incredible.'

He started to talk to his colleagues and the head of the label, Bogdan Roščić, about Igor, about the unusually intense interpretation, about the concentration in the room, about the way Igor sat at the piano, how he made contact with the audience. A kind of communication that you don't get in concerts every day.

Cybinski started to do some research into Igor; he tailed him, went to his next concert, this time in the Kleiner Saal of the Konzerthaus on the Gendarmenmarkt in Berlin: in October 2011, with a programme of pieces all in D minor. A passacaglia by Johann Caspar von Kerll, the Bach Chaconne in the Brahms version for the left hand, Beethoven's Tempest Sonata, in the second part some things by Liszt, as an encore the transcription of 'Isolde's *Liebestod*' from *Tristan und Isolde* by Richard Wagner.

It was a good piece of timing. Cybinski bought tickets for himself and two senior colleagues at Sony, and finagled a meeting: for lunchtime on the day of the concert, sitting outside at a restaurant opposite the Konzerthaus. Igor was on time, but he was tense; he seemed reserved and sceptical. Cybinski and Igor had met briefly, and now Cybinski's colleagues took over the conversation.

What was he interested in musically?

He was in contact with a contemporary American composer, a Communist called Frederic Rzewski, and one day he wanted to play his set of variations on 'The People United Will Never Be Defeated!' – and ideally record it. And of course the big classical pillars of the repertoire, Beethoven, Bach.

Chopin?
No, please not.

Mozart?

Why not tonight's programme – Kerll, Bach, Busoni, Liszt, all in D minor?
Well, then. Sure, why not.

What else was he interested in?

It's the question of the secondary themes with which – if it came to a contract – marketing could add value to the artist and make him interesting.

He saw himself as a very political, very committed person, Igor said. He wanted to express himself, he wanted to adopt positions, he was immediately affected by all the questions on the social and political agenda. The financial crisis, the Greek crisis, the climate disaster. For that reason, he wouldn't be quiet, but loud; he would raise his voice.

After the meeting Cybinski was waiting with his colleagues at Französische Strasse U-Bahn station, and one of his colleagues said only: 'That guy's not marketable.'

That evening Cybinski came alone to the concert.

#

Igor didn't fit the pattern that the record company was looking for. The pianists that sell are young people, both male and female, who also speak to the pop crowd and look good in photographs. Not people who are plainly reflective, who might look interesting, but not classically good looking, who have crazy ideas, and who talk a lot and quickly.

Completely independent of what happens at the piano.

The goal is: what classical musician are you most likely to get on the prime-time Saturday evening programme, into the glossy magazines, into the mass media, to reach a non-academic middle class with a lot of purchasing power? The pattern: the type of person who has already had success should be replicated.

Igor didn't seem to be anything for the broad masses.
But someone who reached the core target group – people who were interested in music for music's sake.

'I was always sure: people would find him incredibly fascinating as a pianist', Cybinski says. Anyone who was interested in a standard-setting interpretation of the canonical masterpieces and beyond would be unable to ignore Igor's recordings, in terms of what he had to say: a pianist who made everyone feel they were being personally addressed.

In the discussions with Sony about which new artists should be signed, Anselm Cybinski became more and more enthusiastic.

Again and again Igor was dropped from the list.

Again and again Cybinski expressed his enthusiasm. Explained why he absolutely belonged on the programme, raved about the concert in the Konzerthaus in October, after the lunch they had had together. He raved about the way Igor shaped sounds and actually orchestrated his works while playing, so that for example in the Liszt you thought you could hear a clarinet, not metaphorically, but really a clarinet – because Igor's playing made the sound of the orchestra so real that the clarinet made perfect sense at that point. He raved about Igor's talent for spreading out tone colours while ensuring that the composition didn't lose its balance, its energy and its rhythmical compactness.

He said it once, twice, three times, four times, five times.

Some of his colleagues were already rolling their eyes; the head of the department laughed, impressed by his stubbornness. But what about the pianist?

'It was clear that Igor wasn't the kind of person you'd be able to make an accessible album of concert favourites with, or who would be particularly willing to compromise on these matters.'

When a major label thinks about what a pianist can record – it's Bach, Chopin, maybe Mozart, Beethoven. Liszt? The B minor sonata at a pinch, the first piano concerto, the *Liebestraum* of course, but everything else? Even the Transcendental Études are too cumbersome. If someone rules out certain composers from the off, it's difficult.

But does 'difficult' also mean impossible?

In the end Cybinski said: if we don't at least see him as a possibility, then an Alfred Brendel, a Murray Perahia, a Grigory Sokolov or an Andras Schiff wouldn't have a chance. That's the scale we're talking about here.

#

In the spring of 2021 Bogdan Roščić and Per Hauber travelled from Sony head office to the Ruhr Piano festival in Essen, where Igor was playing in the hall of the Folkwang University: first the twelve Études by Claude Debussy, then the Grandes Études Transcendentales by Liszt, a typical Igor programme.

Afterwards they met at the bar of the Sheraton Hotel. The three of them discussed questions of repertoire for about twenty minutes. Then for two hours about wine, about the writer Friedrich Torberg, about Christian Wulff, who was about to step down as president. 'The whole time I had the feeling: they're seeing me as who I am', Igor says.

The decision was made the same evening: the debut would be the last five Beethoven sonatas, and eventually Igor would record them all.

Cybinski wasn't there. That night Roščić sent a message to his BlackBerry: spent the whole evening talking about red wine and Friedrich Torberg. We're going to record the five late Beethoven piano sonatas first.

\#

One morning in November 2012 Cybinski collected Igor from his hotel. The previous evening he had given a concert, and there was a party afterwards. They walked together along the Lützow embankment to the Steinway building to choose a grand piano for the recordings of the first album.

Igor sat down at the piano at nine o'clock and played the first movement of the Opus 101 sonata, without playing a single note beforehand. The effect was immediate. Tempo marking: *Etwas lebhaft und mit der innigsten Empfindung* (Somewhat lively, and with the deepest sensitivity).

After four and a half minutes Igor had found his piano.

'Anselm became my producer, and of course Anselm was much more than a producer to me. We spoke on the phone three times a day; I was always bothering him at work. And then we recorded those Beethoven sonatas together. It was a fantastic time.'

Beethoven's last five piano sonatas – a debut album with that programme isn't just a risk; more than anything it's an impertinence. It's the antithesis of the 'One-doesn't-do-that' attitude with which Igor was so often confronted. A provocation by Igor, but even more a provocation by the label to the industry.

These pieces are usually played by pianists twice as old as Igor, at the end of a fulfilled career.

Like every debut album, however, it was a bet that had previously been made on other pianists, and which wasn't always successful. If the pianist delivers, if – as the phrase has it – he shifts some units, things will carry on, and if not, then he's not strong enough. In terms of the programme, you could hardly start higher up, and consequently have further to fall. Total risk.

The recordings went well, and they went quickly. When Igor recorded the Sonata Opus 11, the last of the thirty-two, he had played it only once before in concert. 'But it felt right. It was mine.'

It could have gone incredibly wrong. But it didn't go wrong.

#

A new day, some time in April. Igor's mood was convivial. He was giving a concert in Hanover the next day. The NDR Radio Philharmonic was celebrating its birthday, and he was playing a Mozart piano concerto as a serenade. Without an audience.

But that was still a few hours off.

– After talking about the past last time, now let's talk about the present.

Igor's mood darkened.

– For how many years ahead have you had to cancel dates?

– You can't ask the question that way! Only May has been really cancelled so far. So: Everything in May, almost everything in

June, a lot in July. Salzburg in August is the great unknown. The rest is in the air, we have no idea.

– Would you rather more was cancelled now so that you know where you are?

– Yes and no. I'd rather have some clear statements, of course. But I don't want a totalitarian system either. Quite honestly: I'm wavering. Every day I see the situation a bit differently. That's never been a thing in my life before – from one day to the next I'm not allowed to be who I want to be.

Igor stretches out on the sofa and balances the iPad on his knees. We're talking by video conference.

– A year ago I said in an interview that playing the piano isn't enough for me; I don't just want to be the man who strikes the keys. I wouldn't phrase it like that these days. Now that I'm not allowed to live that life and share my music with other people...

– You also told me in Café Einstein a few weeks ago that you think music on its own can't do anything.

– In political terms it can't, that's right.

– And socially? You see what's happening with your living-room concerts.

– I've never disputed that. I've always been aware that you can move people emotionally, that you can change an atmosphere. But I'm learning a bit more now. None of that is new to me. I've never had to miss playing concerts. Now I miss it.

– On your birthday in the Elbphilharmonie you said you had a sense that something was coming to an end. Since then we've talked about a lot of things, but not about the present: can you tell me what's happened since then?

– I can't tell you in a sentence: my whole plan for my life has vaporized.

– What do you mean?

– I define myself – and regulate myself – via other people. I'm not so great with myself on my own. I tend to like going away from myself rather than towards myself if I'm not feeling great. Then I know: at times like that there are places I can go to. If I feel trapped at home, which happens very often, I know: there's a café where I can go and sit. I can visit friends, I can go to the station and take the train to a different city, all of those things. I have certain strategies – call it distraction; for me it isn't a distraction. It belongs to me. And right now, none of that is possible. I try to compensate for that and somehow pass the time. For a few weeks now I've been telling everybody, ok, fine, now I'll learn to cook. But I can't convince myself that I'm really interested in it. I can just eat raw vegetables all day and I'd be equally happy with that. I need other things in my life apart from that. But all those other things are gone right now.

– When do you think they'll come back? Do you think they'll ever come back?

– I'm sure that there will be a time after Covid. But what state we'll be in when we get there, what structures will still be in place – I'm not a futurologist.

– Was this feeling, this lack, also your reason for launching the house concerts?

– Yes – the sense of urgency, the feeling of necessity. The fact that I can't just sit at the piano. I'm also alone in the concert hall in the afternoon, but then I knew that two floors above me people are sitting in the office and I can go on working for five hours in peace. But I can't work alone at home. I know that if I have no prospect of playing for other people, I'll stop practising. The house concerts are existentially important to me; they really do save my psyche.

– Are the house concerts more demanding than other concerts? Or less demanding?

– I don't differentiate. I see them the same as every other concert; I play them exactly like that as well. I really don't care about how demanding they are. The coffee-roaster from the café downstairs, who is currently taking about 15 per cent of what he normally gets – he's still allowed to go on being a coffee-roaster. My friend Georg can work. You can work. A lot of people are working on reduced hours and yet they're still somehow bound up with a structure.

A pianist who can't put on piano recitals and share his music with other people isn't actually a pianist any more. I don't want to make myself sound worse off than I am. I'm doing ok, I have a financial buffer, I have enough to eat, I can pay the rent. But emotionally I can't go on paddling for ever. Sorry, I've run out of puff today.

– Have you found an answer to the question of what your next big project is going to be?

– Reconstruction.

– What does that mean?

– Honest answer: I don't know. But: I'd rather play for five people than for nobody. And if the pandemic means that we slip into a recession, then that will affect our industry just as much as any other. Unfortunately, I'm sure some places I love a lot will disappear, and I will help to build them up again if I can. And before you ask, I have absolutely no idea what that means.

#

In the spring of 2013 Igor summoned his courage and decided to end his collaboration with the Harrison Parrott agency.

'We weren't communicating any more. We stopped speaking the same language. I'm incredibly grateful that they were there for four years. Good things happened. But in the end, we didn't want the same thing.'

He tormented himself for a long time with the decision. He discussed the matter with colleagues; he called friends from the industry and asked: who is there, where should I go? In the end the name Jack Mastroianni came up, an impresario from New York who works mostly with opera singers. Years ago he took under his wing a young woman who was supposed to be an exceptional talent. Her name: Kristin Schuster.

#

In the summer of 2013, Igor met the violinist Julia Fischer at the Mecklenburg-Vorpommern Festival.

She was a little older than him, but she already had 25 years of stage experience under her belt, and, unlike Igor, she was extremely successful.

The meeting was very important to Igor – above all because, without needing to give it too much thought, she asked some very painful questions.

One of those questions: how do you actually work with your agency?

'I had no answer', Igor says. 'Without that question I would probably not have had the strength to break away.'

She managed to throw him into confusion with a few words – by realistically assessing his situation.

'There are a lot of people who say I play the piano well. I've absolutely never been in their situation of looking at me from the outside. If someone says I'm having this amazing career, then I say, "Ok, thank you very much", but I don't feel it that way. And all of a sudden Julia comes along and says, 'In three or four years you'll be right at the top." I'd just played a lot of concerts in a whole lot of small towns – and I just thought: What the hell makes you think that?'

Igor knew what he could do. But he also knew what he couldn't do.
And the experiences of the past five years had left an impression.

'Of course I wanted to have a career, but I wanted a lot more than that. I wanted to do what's important to me. I've always wanted to live an everyday life for five or six people at the same time. I was a pianist. I slowly became an activist. I wanted to understand the internet. I wanted to do sport. I wanted to lose weight, be well dressed, have as many twitter followers as possible – all at once. And I still want everything all at once. I'm not a pianist who just wants to have a career and that's that.'

Julia Fischer told him about her manager, Kristin Schuster. And she arranged a meeting.

A short time later the three met up in a small concert hall in Grünwald in Munich, where Julia Fischer was recording a CD. Kristin Schuster, who lived in New York, just happened to be in Munich.

During a pause in the recording, Igor sat down at the piano and played, without preparing a note, the Hammerklavier Sonata.

'Because I could', Igor says. 'And also because I felt like it and because I'm a loudmouth. I just thought; bring it on!'

When playing, he accidentally broke the white-gold ring in which he'd had the motto from the Missa Solemnis engraved: *Von Herzen möge es wieder zu Herzen gehen*. May it go once more from heart to heart. It got stuck on a key.

'I'd expected a lot of things that afternoon', Kristin Schuster says, 'but not one of the most difficult works in the piano literature, without announcement or preparation, interpreted with such presence, urgency and refusal to compromise, for an audience of two. For me the matter was clear very quickly. Even before the ring broke in two.'

After the concert they both went to a pavement café in Grünwald with plastic chairs and stick-on table cloths, where there was cappuccino with whipped cream and cocoa powder and Hawaiian toasties on the menu.

It was a phase when Igor wore suits with pocket handkerchiefs, hats and long umbrellas. 'Igor was very definitely nonstandard', Kristin Schuster says. 'It's a happy coincidence that someone can play the piano like that and is also a person you can deal with.'

A month after the release date of Igor's debut album, the two began their collaboration.

'There's no template for Igor's career', Kristin Schuster says; 'there's no template for any artist. And that's true of Igor three times over.'

She had a look at Igor's diary, established that the USA didn't appear on his map, and arranged his debut in New York within a year, while Igor was performing a series of previously arranged concerts in Mecklenburg-Vorpommern. Asia was missing too, although Igor had performed there many times. 'He had', Kristin says, 'been touring below his level for some time.'

She started working, planning and formulating goals strategically with Igor. She brought him together with organizers who understood what made him tick and what his interests were.

Unlike in many large agencies, she wasn't interested in sending Igor into the circus ring as often as possible in as short a time as possible. On the contrary: from now on requests for concerts that were no trouble for Igor, but which also neither stimulated him in terms of content nor stretched him artistically, were refused.

'The meeting with Kristin was one of the most important chance meetings of my life', Igor says. 'We're quite symbiotic in many respects.'

The manner of their collaboration does not correspond to the usual working mode between artist and management, in which one person's main job is to ensure that another person travels from concert to concert, claims successes as their own and chalks failures up to everybody else.

'Kristin is unbelievably intelligent and a thousand times more cultured than I am', Igor says. 'Certainly, I'm the one who ends up sitting at the piano on the stage. But artistically we work on the same level.'

Once he phoned her up, completely thrilled about the idea of commissioning a work from the composer Steve Reich. She listened to his enthusiasm, then took the idea so cleanly apart for a quarter of an hour that Igor was almost more enthusiastic about the demolition of the plan than he had been about the idea itself.

Igor didn't just tolerate her contradiction. He relied on it, or even more: he actually hoped for it.

At many concerts she was in the audience, in Germany, in the USA, anywhere in the world. Of course she used the trips to make contacts, negotiate contracts, organize new performances. Primarily, though, she came for the concert. She came for Igor.

'Every door I've been able to open, every time he's stood in for somebody else, every debut – he used every single one of those opportunities unhesitatingly and with flying colours. I could rely on him 100 per cent. That's the biggest present for a manager: to know that the artist is hungry and pulling his weight – that he's a partner who trusts you completely, and who you can trust completely too.'

'I couldn't do it without Kristin', Igor says. 'And I don't want to either. And if she tells me next week that she's putting together a programme of classical music for Burger King on the moon – ok, I'm switching to Burger King.'

\#

The obvious idea for the American debut of a European pianist would be a concert in the Recital Room at Carnegie Hall.

Kristin Schuster drew the attention of Alex Poots, director of the Park Avenue Armory at the time, to Igor. Poots immediately understood who he had in front of him. He invited Igor to the Armory Drill Hall for a concert in front of an audience of 120. In the auditorium were critics from all the important newspapers and magazines, including the *New York Times* and the *New Yorker*. After the concert Poots came to Igor's dressing room, congratulated him and asked: 'what have you always wanted to play?'

'*Mantra* by Stockhausen', Igor said.

'Seriously?' Poots said. 'Did you know that Stockhausen and I were friends?'

Nothing came of the plan to perform the work. But once again Igor had found a person who saw more in him from the first moment than he saw in himself.

Poots introduced Igor to the performance artist Marina Abramovic. Igor flew to join her in London, and she invited him long after midnight to play the Hammerklavier Sonata in a crowded pub. Then they decided to work together. The result was a performance in which the audience sat for a while in darkness and total silence before Igor played the Goldberg Variations on a grand piano in the middle of the auditorium. The performance ran for three weeks, almost every evening. It was Igor's second project in New York, and it brought him to international attention.

Thorsten Schmidt travelled in from Heidelberg for the premiere. He was followed a few days later by Igor's best friend Hannes Malte Mahler, who had studied with Abramovic in Braunschweig and hadn't seen her for years.

'A lot of things came full circle here', Igor says, 'and a lot more had only just got going. I could also tell stories similar to the one about Alex Poots about John Gilhooly in London, who invited me to perform a complete Beethoven cycle at the Wigmore Hall late in 2020. Or Markus Hinterhäuser who, two years before he took over as artistic director of the Salzburg Festival, invited me with the question: Igor, tell me quite honestly, what do you want to play?'

\#

Yet another day. Igor is sitting on the sofa in his flat, drowning in boredom, and at the same time barely able to sit still, he's so thirsty for action. He doesn't know where to put himself, there's nothing to do: why prepare for concerts that aren't going to happen. He's both too little and too much for himself.

Perhaps for the first time in his career he finds himself powerless before an obstacle, eye to eye with a problem bigger than he is.

He has failed many times in his life, defeated by people and circumstances but also, from his own perspective, by himself.

Whatever it is that wasn't working, it can – at least in his weaker moments – be read as being down to him. As not being good enough.

This time there's really nothing he can do about it. And that makes it harder rather than easier to bear. He knows how to cope with his own failure.

No one can do anything about it. And to top it all no one knows how to deal with it. No colleague, no politician, no friend, there's no right way of dealing with it, only a whole lot of wrong ones.

Igor puts his iPad down on the table.

– How are you today, Igor?

– I don't know.

– What are we going to talk about?

– I don't know. You tell me.

– Maybe, by way of distraction, about Beethoven.

– Nice distraction.

– The piece with which you introduced yourself to a wider public was the first of the last five piano sonatas, no. 28. The instruction for the first movement reads: rather lively and with the deepest sensitivity. Listening to it, it's clear after only a few bars: this sounds different from the way other pianists play it. More direct, more straightforward, more personal. Was that your intention? Did you listen to recordings by your colleagues and wonder: how can I distinguish myself – a bit faster here, a bit louder there? How did you find out what you wanted to express with the piece?

Igor exhales.
– I didn't.

– What?

– That's not how I think. I've never worked on an interpretation in my life.

He sits up.

– An interpretation – I mean, what the hell is that supposed to be? I play music as intuitively as I can, I go here and there, I keep changing routes the whole time, and at the same time try to stay honest, open and authentic.

But at the same time I can't work on a version that then is and remains my interpretation – I have no idea how you would do that. I have a thousand thoughts in my head when I'm playing, and I'm thinking about a billion things at the same time. And I allow in new impulses and ideas.

When I play a piece today it's completely different from the way I played it a month ago. As soon as I play a piece it's automatically my interpretation from today. And tomorrow it's the one from tomorrow, and the day after tomorrow the one from the day after tomorrow.

I've stripped layers away. That's my way of working. I keep trying to press on to the core. At the beginning it's easy, then it gets harder, because the layers get more and more delicate.

I'm only interested in how I get it to sound like me.

In the old days I used armour. I didn't leave the house without a suit, tie and handkerchief in my top pocket. That's all gone. I don't need a lot of possessions; I don't need to hoard. I don't need discussions about concert hall acoustics.

I try to strip away layers until all that's left is me.

Every day all over again. That's what work means for me. I want to make myself as light as possible and as transparent as possible. I want to let in the here and now. If that means a total mental vacancy: then that's just how it is. If I have a billion thoughts in my head: that's ok too.

And just when I have the feeling that I'm as transparent as

possible, I'm not allowed to play. I've never felt as good at the piano as I do now.

I go to the piano in the state of mind that I happen to be in at the time, regardless of what happens. It's right. Stripping layers away also means that I don't try to depict anything other than what I am. I don't try to play myself off against myself to reach an interpretation that's going to be valid over and over again. I play what I play, and trust it. I just accept my condition.

Of course that doesn't mean that I don't stick to the instructions in the sheet music – of course I stick to that, sometimes more, sometimes less. But if in a concert I play a different tempo in a particular passage, or leave out a sforzando – so what! Is anybody going to die? No. Is anybody going to have to declare bankruptcy? No. Will anybody notice? Maybe – if he plays the sonata, he can do the sforzando to his heart's content.

To allow yourself this attitude, of course, you need to know the piece really well. Because if you were to pin me down, I would know exactly where there's a forte and where there isn't. But once again: it's my piece. And if I stick to everything that composer wrote, it's still my piece. I can prove it. Watch this.

He pans around the apartment with the iPad: the kitchen door, the wall with the painting by Hannes Malte Mahler, the grand piano, the windows.

– Do you see anyone here?

– No.

– Yes, exactly. Bad luck, there's nobody here. It's just my piece. I sometimes wonder why we even need to talk about it, it's obvious. You know, I like it when things are simple. Easy, uncomplicated, to the point.

– Can all pieces become your pieces or are there exceptions?

– Sure, I've also played pieces that turned out to be mistakes. But only ever once. After that I was incredibly unhappy, and that was that.

– How can you tell that a piece isn't your piece?

– Counter-question: how can you tell that someone doesn't like you?

– Do you have an example?

– The Scriabin piano concerto. I don't think that I don't like the piece, generally speaking. But I shouldn't play it. It doesn't say anything to me; it has nothing to do with me. L'art pour l'art. I can't do it, it's not mine.

– What else is there?

– Not so much. The Messiaen quartet. I don't even enjoy learning the notes. I notice it's not working.

And I often feel the same way about Chopin. I really do love him. But when I sit down at the piano and start playing, I feel awful. That may change one day, but I'm not there yet.

– But what bothers you about Chopin?

– Nothing bothers me. I bother myself. I can't get it the way I want it and I don't understand why. Maybe it's an illusion, maybe it's better than I think. But as long as I can't get it the way I want it, it gets on my nerves.

#

The life that Igor led up to the release of his debut CD can be summed up in a single sentence: he does what he wants.

First of all because the people around him – parents, teachers, friends – made it possible for him. Later, because nobody else apart from parents, teachers and friends seemed to be interested in him. By the time that changed, he would not be deflected from his course of following his own instinct rather than the demands of other people. And when he enjoyed his first successes, he considered himself validated: clearly it was right not to make concessions for the sake of success.

From outside that didn't necessarily look so nice.

'Assuming responsibility for other people wasn't my thing. For a very long time I just did what I wanted. For other people I was the guy who played the piano, period.'

That changed overnight in 2014. A year after the release of Igor's first album of the last five Beethoven piano sonatas, Igor's mother fell ill. Cancer.

Igor decided to look after her. Only a few people knew about it, but the ones who did were surprised by Igor's reaction.

'I remember a woman friend saying to me: "The idea that you should not only see but fulfil such a role of responsibility, you of all people?" All of a sudden I had shed one skin and pulled on a new one.'

For a year and a half, almost two years, Igor accompanied his mother to chemotherapy, visited her in hospital, and – if at all possible – went back to his family in Hanover after every concert.

'Outwardly nobody noticed, I barely told anyone. Those were two intense, very difficult years. I trained myself to be extremely tough. I knew I had to function. I played a huge number of concerts that year, I barely slept.'

His mother's illness coincided with the moment when his career finally took off. He played 108 concerts in one year, a greater burden than he could bear.

He overreached himself.
He was aware of it.
But carried on anyway.

'That time changed everything for me. I lost sleep. I lost all sense of what my space really was. I'm only aware of that in retrospect. I had a beautiful apartment here, a lovely old building with a little balcony. In my apartment were: my grand piano, some unpacked moving cases, a bed and a cupboard. I didn't once go out onto the balcony. Hang on, no, that's not true, I did once – with Hannes, my best friend. We drank half a bottle of champagne. That was a wonderful evening.'

His best friend Hannes picked him up as best he could. So did a few other friends, 'otherwise I wouldn't have managed', he says. 'Outwardly at the time I was the kind of person who had a career – and inside there was nothing at all, just hardness, unfortunately. I say "unfortunately", but I don't regret it. It's just how my life was. But I don't want that any more.'

When it was clear that his mother was on the way back to health and recovering quite quickly, Igor made the impromptu decision to go to Berlin.

#

On New Year's Day 2016, he relocated to Berlin.

Spring came, then summer, and gradually Igor felt as if he could breathe more freely again. Then one morning his phone rang, when Igor was rehearsing with Simon Bode for a performance in Ludwigsburg.

Hannes was dead.
A cycling accident.
Igor collapsed.

It was another two and a half years before he came to terms with it.

'Outwardly I carried on working. I became just a tiny bit harder on myself. I played sport every day, I kept learning new repertoire, I played one concert after another, I didn't allow myself to lie down when I was tired.'

The months after Hannes' death are the time when Igor became more and more political.

Those were the months following the day when a majority in the United Kingdom voted to leave the EU.

It was the autumn when Donald Trump was elected US President.

In the spring Igor had been with Georg Diez in Idomeni, the refugee camp on the Greek–Macedonian border. The impressions were still fresh in his mind.

'I've always, always gone into action, I haven't left myself any room. Those moments shape my whole life. I want more and more! To live, see, experience, learn more. And then of course there's a great danger of simply leaving behind other people who are important to you. For a long time I hadn't been particularly good at turning around to other people and asking: are you actually coming with me?'

#

'You can tell without any difficulty, I'm not Igor Levit, he'll be here shortly', President Frank-Walter Steinmeier said into Igor's phone on 2 April. On that day the tripods were set up not in his apartment but in the Bellevue Palace. Steinmeier had invited Igor to perform today's house concert from his apartment – as a sign of gratitude.

'I'm one of the many people who love the house concerts that he's been giving for many days since the start of the Covid crisis', Steinmeier says, sitting on the piano stool at the grand piano. 'Igor Levit, a great artist who tells us something about the power of music. Who tells us how important art is, and shows us that music can be consoling. But that's not all, because he also reminds us that the situation of many artists is currently far from easy, many artists are in poverty, they have no opportunities to perform, no concerts, no productions. And because many are in poverty, they also need our support. He reminds us of this in his house concerts, not from his home today, though, but here, the interior of the Bellevue Palace. Like you, I will shortly follow the concert on livestream, and I wish you some relaxation in this tense time.'

Then Igor appears on camera, sits down on the now empty piano stool and clears his throat.

'I am delighted, and thank President Frank-Walter Steinmeier for this invitation; it's a great honour. I'm just very grateful to be here, in the Bellevue Palace.'

He plays the programme of the first house concert, Piano Sonata Opus 53 in C Major, the Waldstein Sonata.

'I just want to say a few words', Igor goes on. 'Why this piece? For me this is the most life-affirming, the most edifying, cheering, inspiring piano music there is. It's a piece that brings inspiration, that brings happiness. That hugs you. This work is a great gift. The heartbeat of the first movement, the intensity, the embrace of the second, and the hymn to life of the unparalleled third movement – it is with this hymn to life and this work that I would like to be with you today.'

Then he plays. Not quite as radiantly and commandingly as he did six months ago in the Elbphilharmonie. But his playing is also less categorical and driven than it was three weeks ago in his living room – and with a better tone.

Here too, he is playing mostly for himself.

A few days previously he himself would have found it hard to imagine being here today rather than at home.

Even though, if it had been up to him, he would rather have been somewhere else entirely.

#

During the house concerts Igor tweets:

'In this dimension, so existential to me, I have perhaps never felt the actually life-saving significance of music and notes as much as I do now. Everything feels new. Thank you for letting me share it with you. It really does contain an inner glow. See you tomorrow.'

#

The grand piano that Igor plays at home once belonged to the Swiss pianist Edwin Fischer, a celebrated interpreter of Beethoven. Igor calls the instrument 'Edwin'. It was made in 1923. Thomas Hübsch, the piano tuner who gets the instrument ready for him before his concerts, has refurbished it. It's one of three grand pianos in Igor's fleet.

Before 'Edwin', 'Lulu' stood in his living room. An American couple gave it to him on one of the cruises. Igor played, and over dinner he chatted with his neighbours. They asked him: what does a pianist actually need in order to have a career? Igor said: good teachers, good people around him, a good piano. – Like that one over there on the stage? – Yes, one like the one over there on the stage. A few days later they said to him: We've decided to put a piano at your disposal. Initially it was on loan from a foundation, but now it belongs to Igor – the name Lulu is a reference to the Alban Berg opera, and to the instrument's wilfulness.

Igor was still living with his parents, he didn't know what to do with it, and in the end he lodged it in an old people's home in the neighbourhood, where it didn't age well because more than once the ambient temperature was wrong. 'Lulu' moved with him to his first apartment in Hanover, and was lifted over the balcony by crane. And when Igor had to leave his first Berlin apartment on Strassburger Strasse because the landlord needed to use it himself, he had it moved to the Steinway grand piano store in Berlin. The storage capacities were limited. When his colleague Andras Schiff needed access, Lulu had to move out of storage – and ended up in a recording studio in Französisch-Buchholz.

In the meantime Igor had bought a third grand piano, 'Monk', after Thelonious Monk, whom Igor admires for the clarity and directness of his tone. It was on this one that he played the Beethoven sonatas in Hamburg, Salzburg and Berlin, but by now 'Monk' was stored in Hamburg, and couldn't stay there for ever.

Several friends had offered to accommodate one of his instruments in their homes. He still hadn't made his mind up.

#

It was only much later, in Salzburg, that Igor clearly understood the true importance of the house concerts.

The thing that made them so special was a factor so obvious that one would not immediately see it as special: their simplicity.

Igor needed two smartphones with tripods, access to the platforms Twitter and Instagram, an instrument – and an audience that he reached directly via social media. What he didn't need were the usual tools and aids of the classical music business – programme planning, marketing, staging, creating attention. In other words: what he didn't need was the classical music business. The routines and rituals, the allocation of roles. The agencies. The power structures.

Everyone who usually decides whether a piece is worth listening to right now and why, whether an artist is interesting, whether it's worth paying attention to a particular programme, whether a musician is worth the money or overvalued many times over, whether a concert was good or not – in the case of the house concerts they were only a few spectators among many.

The decision about whether a programme is interesting or not was now made entirely by Igor and the audience, each on his own.

Igor played what he felt like, without asking for permission.
Anyone who wanted to listen could.
And they were at liberty to interpret the programme as they wished.

The only thing that distinguished them from conventional concerts: nobody made any money from them, not even Igor himself. But even here there were ways and means – classical ticket sales wouldn't work, but other models might.

For the classical music business, particularly the agencies which had now become irrelevant, this success was an insult – a greater one than the crisis in the recording industry. In those days only music had freed itself from the commercial supporting medium, and now the artist and his audience were threatening to emancipate themselves completely.

As the year progressed, the arts pages made the extent of the insult all the more apparent to Igor.

For Igor himself, on the other hand, the step was a huge boost to his self-confidence, and with it his sense of his own independence from external judgement.

And that was what told him how dependent he had been until then.

When we talk about the house concerts over lunch in Salzburg, Igor lowers his knife and fork in reaction to the question of what he learned about himself during that time.

'I'll tell you something now – don't just take it at face value. If you were to write it down, I don't know if anybody would believe me, but I don't care any more.

'During that time – perhaps for the first time – I became aware that I wasn't a fake. That I'm not just pretending. For the first time I myself believed that I was a pianist.'

You have to let that sink in for a moment.

'For the first time I didn't feel small on the stage, I felt good and strong.

And for the first time I understood something emotionally that I had actually known for a long time: I can't control how the music reaches my listeners – and what it unleashes in them.

I can only control the notes at the moment when they are produced, I've been working on that for decades, I can strike a key in such a way that the note sounds sad or cheerful to me, brave or lost. But how it sounds in your ears: I have no control over that at all. And then I also mustn't act as if I did. That might sound odd, but it gives you an incredible freedom. The only thing I knew for sure was: something good comes out of it. And someone other than me is responsible for it.

It has nothing to do with the aura of the auditorium, with the aura of the work, of the instrument. It's all down to me. Apart from me there was nothing there. No framework, no rituals, no moment when the lights in the auditorium are lowered and I come on stage in a suit and bow. Everything that usually indicates that a concert is something special – the pianist has to be good or else he wouldn't be on stage in the first place – disappears.

I didn't take my clothes off, I didn't lower my trousers, not at all, but in those house concerts I was simply me. I was at home, dressed as I wanted to be, I said what I wanted to say, so openly, as transparently, as honestly, and in as relaxed a way as I wanted. And without a hint of ulterior motives.

I adopted this plan for the first time – and it adopted me. I had the sense to recognize that this was what needed to be done right now.

I said: now you can see who I am. That made a mark a thousand times deeper in a human, political and artistic sense than all statements and programmes put together. For me that was a big and beautiful lesson.

For the first time it was clear to me why I was doing that, both rationally and emotionally. For the first time I didn't have a sense that I had to deliver – I had something to give.

In the end there was only me. Feeling that was the most beautiful thing of all. For the first time I had a sense I hadn't just happened at random.

I threw out all the rules in existence. I just showed myself. To myself, not least. And the fact that it happened like that, that was the best thing.

I did what I wanted. I've done that in the past too, but now I'd sensed and understood it.

'I very much hope that this feeling stays with me.'

#

The issue of self-doubt is one of the things that you can only understand if you spend a lot of time with Igor and observe him over time.

Igor knows, of course, that he can play the piano. He believes people because they've been telling him time and again for ten, fifteen, twenty years.
But he's still not convinced.

'I'm deeply sensitive. I approach things with the same enthusiasm for their content as before, and I react with the same insecurity if someone steps up to me with a raised forefinger and tells me all the things that aren't ok. All that I want from other people in life is to be seen. Just to be seen.'

This shouldn't be confused with the productive mania that all good pianists have, and which keeps their engine running: the constant terror of not being good enough, of chasing after an ideal and never reaching it.

Igor is driven by something else. A doubt that stopped being a doubt a long time ago. It's a conviction that deserves to be called rock-solid. A constant stumbling block.

He thinks he can't do it. It's not enough.

And that also helps to explain why he sounds the way he sounds: he is playing against doubt.

And he doesn't just play against it; he lives against it too. Hence the impression that Igor makes things a lot harder for himself than he needs to.

It isn't easy.

And it isn't made any easier by the fact that Igor knows he can only do everything that he does as long as he is free of doubt when he sits at the piano.

\#

Yet another day. Igor looks tired. The American tour that he was supposed to do in May has been in danger for a long time, and now it becomes clear that it's completely impossible.

The days merged into one another. Igor played house concert after house concert, and spent the rest of the day finding a structure that worked without the important cornerstones of his previous life – professional trips, private trips, spontaneous meetings with friends in cafés, concerts. Meanwhile Kristin Schuster was trying to postpone concert dates, first once, then again. Managers of musicians are usually only paid for the concerts that take place. The musicians themselves too.

– How are you, Igor?

– I don't know.

– Did you hear the interview with the Austrian President on ORF?

– No. Any good? Hang on a second.

He opens Twitter, looks for a while, then Alexander van der Bellen starts talking out of his iPhone speaker.

– Makers of art and culture don't just want approval; they also want financial security. I think that's completely fine, it's right, but why is it right? Art and culture, and I cannot stress this enough, have an inherent value beyond all commercial exploitation. Whether it be in literature, in music, in visual art or in any other field. That's one thing. And the other is: we, non-creators of culture, experience art essentially through interaction. Regardless of whether we go to an art gallery, whether we hear a piece of music, whether we're at home, whether we're in a larger event, in a concert hall, for example, or whether we go to the opera. So for me, for example, I can't forget having had the opportunity to see a performance of *Salomé* at the Salzburg Festival. And I'm not at all an opera fan. But it simply blew me away. That's the second point, and the third point is: art and culture also have a commercial significance, for other people. Urban tourism, particularly in Vienna and Salzburg, but also in other regions, also thrives on art and culture. People don't just come to see St Stephen's Cathedral, beautiful as it is; they go to the opera as well.'

– 'So you also see culture as an economic issue', the presenter says.

– 'Yes, definitely that too. But the emphasis is on *too*, so perhaps you need to argue for its importance. But it's important for me to stress art and culture as values in themselves, and as a value for us, the audience. The people who listen and watch, and who bring their enthusiasm and admiration, whether it's in the cinema or the theatre or wherever.'

– 'Thank you very much, Mr President.'

Igor exhales and rubs his eyes for a long time.

– And what was so brilliant about that?

– Well, I haven't heard a German politician say anything like that for weeks.

– Oh, you know. No idea, I just don't feel like having one of those 'At last somebody's saying it' conversations. Art and culture are this thing and that thing – people have said that here too. And art and culture as an economic issue

– people have said that here too. But those are two completely different conversations. The question of financial support for this world, once it has been rescued, is raised here too. There are emergency aid programmes, they're small and too late, but however much I might enjoy criticizing politicians, they're doing that in one form or another.

But that doesn't alter the fact that something else isn't happening right now – and there isn't anyone I can hold accountable for that.

At the moment I can't be a musician. I can't appear and perform, without fear, in a room with other people, without fear.

It's not a political problem. The small part that can be politically solved is already being solved. But the much bigger part is not solvable: my life has been brought to an end. The life that I led until March 2020 is over.

Of course there will be concerts again, but how? I find it grotesque to carry on as if the atmosphere didn't matter. It does matter! It matters whether there's a distance of half a metre or four metres between the musicians in an orchestra. To say that the main thing is that we're playing, regardless of how – that's grotesque! The only thing that seems to matter at the moment is the financial rescue of this world, whatever the cost. But there is no 'whatever the cost'. There are costs that can't be covered with money. I don't want consolation either – there's nothing to be consoled for. Those of us who live on music have all been robbed of our livelihood. And once again: it isn't the fault of any politician, it's no one's fault, the time itself is to blame.

And if you were to ask me now: What do you want? I can tell you quite clearly. I want the climate from 10 March back. I would like people who are free to cheer or boo, who hug each other, who are pressed up against each other, who look at each other, who spin each other around. Who have a drink at the interval, raise a glass, celebrate the moment. Right now that isn't possible. And what am I in a world in which that isn't possible? I don't know. Perhaps after the first time I can say it was great because I'm carried by the music. If the music doesn't carry me, then I'm not carrying on with it. But the big question is: If we don't do it, we may as well shut up shop. And I'll say one thing to you: I'm giving up when I get the first call to play at a drive-in. I'm stepping down immediately. I didn't work on a thing for 30 years of my life to play in front of a bunch of cars.

#

On 2 May Igor played the fiftieth house concert. He sat on the piano stool in a black pullover and black jeans; he had his glasses on and addressed a few words to his audience.

'On 12 March I started playing these concerts out of a sense of urgency. It was the urgent need to share. I can't make music without sharing. That doesn't work for me; I can't just do it for me. I've got to know people are listening.

And since that 12th of March the way we've been used to doing things over years and decades obviously doesn't exist any more: places are shut, concert halls are shut, festivals are cancelled. We don't know for how long. We also don't know which places will still be there when we're allowed to start up again. We don't know a thing. What we do know, though: what notes, what sounds, what music can do with us. It can heal. It can help. It doesn't have to. But it can.

But for me those evenings were more healing and more existential than almost anything in my previous life. And I've been making music since before I was three. Up to eight weeks ago I thought I'd experienced some things. And I've never felt distanced from music. But just a note really helping me, tangibly, in a physical sense, the quality of that was something quite new.

And playing here for you every evening and knowing people are listening, knowing you're there, during these weeks, that has very personally given me support, strength and a warm feeling that I can't even describe.

My gratitude to you is boundless, and I mean that literally: boundless.

'I don't know how long this will last, and what it will do to me and to you, and I won't pretend it's easy. But for these last two months I can say: as long as I can think clearly, as long as I live, I will never forget these two months.'

Then he played the Goldberg Variations by Johann Sebastian Bach, 'just under 80 minutes of the most sacred, unbelievable, indescribable music. The work begins exactly as it ends, with the Aria, and between those two poles we experience a journey together. To put it superficially: we go back to where we came from, but as different people. The impressions are different, the feelings are different, the normal is a new normal.'

Two days later Igor stopped the house concerts.

'I miss them', he said a few weeks later. 'I miss the mood, the freedom, the intimacy, the rhythm, the joy of it. I was able to decide half an hour beforehand what I was going to play. But that's not the only reason. I wish I'd enjoyed the concerts even more. Because the awareness of that immense freedom only came later. I wish it had been there from the start.

During that time I wasn't feeling so great, because my mind was elsewhere. I was grieving for my old life, and the concerts were a great help to me with that grief. But at the same time I didn't notice how good a time that actually was. I changed a lot during that period, and I could almost watch myself changing.

I miss that, but it just isn't coming back.

Along the way I thought briefly I didn't have enough repertoire. But then it happened, then something came into being. I once did the calculation: I could have played 100 concerts without really repeating myself.

And the reaction was overwhelming. There were only a few stuffed-shirt comments from colleagues complaining about the sound quality and demanding a perfect grand piano with perfect intonation. But that wasn't what I was after – for me it was important to know that people were sitting listening on the other side of my mobile phone camera. And of course the sound wasn't good, but what would the alternative have been? I didn't deliberately decide against having a perfect grand piano; I was faced with the choice: like this or not at all.'

#

In May, the day after his cancelled debut at Carnegie Hall, Igor is sitting in an old dance hall in Französisch-Buchholz, north of Berlin-Pankow. That morning the Bavarian governor Markus Söder spoke once again at a Covid press conference in Munich about large-scale events, without saying whether he included piano recitals in that, and everyone was tired, uneasy and cautious.

It was the evening after the last house concert.

Igor stopped because he and Kristin Schuster were starting a recording: an album of chorale preludes by Bach and Brahms transcribed by Ferruccio Busoni – and doing the recordings and the house concerts in parallel would have been too much.

The dance hall in Französisch-Buchholz is home to the recording studio where his piano Lulu has been for a few weeks. Here Igor is playing three Beethoven sonatas, including the last one, Opus 111. The recording is going to be transmitted on the website of the Gilmore Festival.

Igor, an hour before the recording, tries somehow to rid the room of its gloomy atmosphere.

'Hey, I've got a joke for you, listen up.
After the murder of Tsar Alexander II the mayor of Kiev invites the grand rabbi in and says: You don't need to come and apologise, I know very well it was one of you lot.
So the rabbi says: Ach, always the same. Always the same. Doesn't matter what I say. For you guys it was always either the chimney sweeps or the Jews.
The mayor says: Hang on, why the chimney sweeps?
And the rabbi says: Well, and why always the Jews?'

Jokes are Igor's way of radically changing a mood; every listener reacts differently, but they all react: some wonder whether it's ok to laugh at a Jewish joke. Others just laugh. And others struggle to understand it.

Igor sits down at the piano and rehearses for a bit, and then the recording begins. For everybody in the room, it's the first notes they've heard on a piano for at least two months.

The debut in the large auditorium at Carnegie Hall is now rescheduled for January 2022.

Afterwards Igor sits down on a red sofa in the corner and says solemnly: 'Ok, I've got something to tell you.'

He has a plan. A livestream, here in this studio, 20 hours, maybe more – he wants to play *Vexations*, a composition by Erik Satie, consisting of a theme and two variations played 840 times. 'The piece is basically my soundtrack right now', Igor says. 'It isn't about anything at all.'

He will play for a day and a night. 'That', Igor says, 'is going to be my artistic hunger strike.'

#

A week before the agreed date, Igor starts having doubts about whether playing *Vexations* was really such a brilliant idea after all.

'Right now I could kick myself; I've got nothing to do but spend 21 hours sitting at the piano. It's yet another typical Igor action: I have an idea, I get it moving and only then think about what it really means. No idea what'll happen. I may run out of patience after an hour.'

But right now he really has nothing else to do.

Vexations is a composition by the Frenchman Erik Satie for whom Igor has a lot of sympathy, because his works can't really be assigned to a particular stylistic era – and it's not even clear if all his works were really meant seriously.

This piece is the best example. A theme, consisting of eighteen notes, two variations each of seventeen harmonies, and the whole thing 840 times, 'an awful lot of repetitions of very few notes', Igor says. 'Really not difficult. Easy-peasy. You could do it yourself if I showed you.'

Above the notes, in French, is the ambiguous instruction: 'In order to play the motif 840 times in succession, it would be advisable to prepare oneself beforehand, and in the deepest silence, by serious immobilities.'

Does that mean that the composer is saying the theme has to be played 840 times? Or is it a joke, the caricature of an instruction that just says: if someone is bad enough to play this 840 times, then don't do it unprepared? There probably wouldn't have been much point asking Erik Satie himself even when he was alive.

Art is free and ungraspable. If it could be grasped, it would no longer be free.

The melody sounds like some casual noodling, a few notes hung together as if at random, not particularly beautiful, and not memorable. In the variations a chord sits on each note, and here again every note could be random. The series makes no harmonic sense and, most importantly: the tension between the notes remains unresolved. The piece has no key and no bars; it is like a meandering feeling of tautness, like the strange knots in a telephone cable that seem to appear out of nowhere and never disappear again. After the first run-through, you're already dying to hear a clear C major chord.

Igor has wanted to play the piece for a long time. He first mentioned it when he took part in Marina Abramovic's performance at the Armory Hall in New York, and later decided to perform the work in front of a live audience. Kristin Schuster talked him out of it, finding the idea too self-referential. Why repeat a senseless melody and two variations for a whole day and night without any notable interval, except to show that you can keep it up. Igor rejected the plan, but he didn't forget it.

Things look different now: for two and a half months the concert halls have been closed, and many artists have had the rug pulled out from under them. While in the good times the significance of art for society wasn't an issue, all of a sudden it seemed to be in doubt. There was the matter of money too, but above all: the point of carrying on. Because no one becomes an artist unless they're convinced that art is worth spending your whole life on. The main problem is not the closure of the concert halls themselves, but the indifference with which it was enforced by the responsible politicians. Which was taken to mean: it's not that important.

Now – unlike with the house concerts, Igor expressly doesn't want to fill that void. He wants to make the gap audible. As a cry of pain from art, that's the idea.

At any rate he must stay below two minutes. If one play takes two minutes, 840 repetitions take 27 hours, not including toilet breaks.

The plan is for 24 hours.
Twenty would be better.

Berlin-Pankow, back in the old dance hall, 30th May, Whit Saturday. The lights are out in the hall, the air outside is mild, it's an extravagantly beautiful day and the birds are singing. At least we've still got them.

Inside the hall the spotlights come on, the grand piano is in the back part of the room, surrounded by partitions, and the set is bathed in honey-coloured light.

The parquet creaks with each step.

At the piano in the half-darkness: the light mixing desk, in the corner a red sofa, at the back end a trestle with a little lamp so that Igor doesn't lose his bearings in the blackness of the stage – and so that none of the assistants trips over a cable. Behind that, a door to the technical area, which will later be closed because the steps creak too loudly. In front of the piano are three cameras, and a fourth hangs from the ceiling. Just out of shot: two toilets with their ceiling lights covered over, one of them for Igor. Will we hear the toilet flush during the recording? Brief commotion; no, as soon as Igor leaves the shot, the sounds goes off.

Half a dozen camera operators, lighting assistants and sound engineers are there, the directors of photography work in shifts, so do the camera operators. In a side room someone is taking care of the streams. Last preparations, tense expectation, nervous anticipation.

The production manager has set up a little camp on the right-hand side wall; if it's really going to go on for 28 hours people are going to need some sleep.
Then Igor arrives, sunglasses, holding a designer chair from his kitchen. 'I thought a chair with a back mightn't be the worst idea.'

He's come up with an ingenious method which he plans to master. Maren Borchers carries a light grey cardboard box to the piano. 'Look, I've brought you something.' In the box are 840 A4 sheets of paper, printed on one side. One page per repetition.

The stack lies on top of the piano, to the right of the music stand. Camera 2 can no longer see Igor, who has disappeared behind the stack.

'What, is that all?' Igor asks. He sits on the kitchen chair and tinkles out a version of the March of the Gladiators, an old circus tune. He breaks off after a few bars. 'Right, I've rehearsed.'

Maren Borchers had insisted that a doctor should be present, and Igor had asked his old friend Olli Rohde if he might be able to drop in. The two know each other via Hannes, and every now and again they go into the mountains on a boys' trip. Olli, an affable, bearded man with a brightly coloured T-shirt and a flat cap, is actually a paediatrician, but so what, a doctor is a doctor. Right now he's fetching provisions from the car: dried fruit and organic chocolate, tuna salad.

'Have we got bananas?'
'Yes, it's beside the piano.'
'What, just the one?'
'Are the dates stoned?'
'No, you can just spit the stones into the piano. Of course they're stoned.'

The speakers crackle; a voice from the director's box says: 'Igor, I know you have a hell of a programme ahead of you, but could you just play two or three repetitions for us?'

Maren Borchers stands nervously on a little veranda outside the kitchen, tapping on her phone. She is worried. Several pianists developed hallucinations while trying to play *Vexations*; one of them saw dragons coming out of the manuscript.

Another half hour.

The production manager comes out onto the terrace.
'Are you feeling ill too?'

'Are you feeling ill?' Maren Borchers asks. 'Are you over-excited?'
'God damn it. Every time.'
'Really? Get out of here! Why?'
'Terrible. Because of the technical side of it.'
Igor, in the background: 'So why are YOU over-excited?

13.48. Igor calls from the piano: 'Can we get started?'

'Would you rather play on the piano stool or on your chair, asks Olli, the paediatrician.
'On the piano stool.'
'Fine.'
'Nah, on the chair after all.'

13.51: 'Can we get going?'
13.52: 'Could we get started now?'
Igor stands in the semi-darkness, stretches his shoulders, rubs the back of his neck with his left hand.

13:53: 'Hello, I want to start playing!'
13.55: Maren Borchers says goodbye. 'So, my dear, have a good trip.' Igor waves and looks serious.

Then everything's quiet for a moment.

13:58: 'And on stage please.'
The production manager claps Igor carefully on the back.

Igor walks into the honey-coloured light, sits down beside the pile of music, straightens the music stand, concentrates briefly and starts.

He takes his time.
Note for note. For note. For note.
First variation.

Theme again.
Second variation.

One minute 40. Exactly 100 seconds. Adds up to 23 hours.

The sheets of music are numbered, and after each pass Igor lets a sheet fall to the floor. He plays effortlessly, without gestures, without expression. First the theme must seep into the consciousness.

Curious that the tune doesn't stay in your head, it doesn't even seem to want to.

13.22: Igor sighs.
13.56: A trill in the main theme.

Otherwise nothing happens. Igor plays, the machines run, time passes.

But what's curious is that it isn't boring.

16.46: Sheet 111. Igor gets to his feet and walks out of shot. Pause, five minutes.

Then, very slowly, he gets back up to speed.

It will go on like that for a few hours now. In fact people could go for a walk, have a nap, get some work done. But it's impossible, you have the feeling you might miss something.

Second pause after sheet 219. Igor steps out of the light and beckons Olli over: 'Hey, that tuna salad, where is it?'

Then back to it, the sheets crash to the floor, the tempo accelerates again, the intensity too, each pass now lasts less than a minute.

Sheet 299, it's a quarter to nine.

Igor gets to his feet, looks into the camera and plays a few times while standing.

Sheet 300, he sits down again.

These are the events that divide up infinity. Igor sighing. Crossing his legs. Eating dates. Drinking water, playing the tune only with his left hand which gives him a few seconds to have a drink or pile on more music.

Just 22.00, not even half-way through.

But strangely: it still isn't boring.

Igor isn't just reeling off the music, he phrases and modulates, he takes the music for what it is: an inordinately long set of variations.

The camera operators switch in two-hour shifts, their colleagues in photographic direction too. The director, who is sitting at the controls, says he gave his mother the Beethoven sonata boxed set for Christmas. He'd never heard of Igor before.

22.10: Igor stands up again, plays standing up, stamps his foot, sings along.

22:18: He sinks wearily into the chair, wipes his eyes.

At 22.24 he just keeps the pedal down, and now the notes don't follow in succession, but instead accumulate into a single great cloud.

No two variations are the same.

22.33: Sheet 420. That's half of it done, much faster than planned.

Igor steps out of shot into the semi-darkness and says: 'This is really something.'

'We're going much quicker than planned', the production manager says.
'Don't count your chickens! The slow movement's coming up.'

The production manager sends one of the camera operators into the kitchen, where the catering is ready for the crew. 'Grab a couple of bits of lasagne, carbohydrates.'
By the time the lasagne is ready, Igor is playing again.
By now the floor is covered with sheets of music.

Just before the next interval, Georg Diez comes into the room; he promised Igor he would drop by. Two other friends are there too, sitting on the sofa, chatting quietly, but not quietly. Igor gives them icy looks from the stage.

His playing becomes flatter, the contours blur, the music sounds more lost, the determination that carried Igor through the last few hours has seeped away.

00.56: 'So I'd have to say, the Satie is slowly getting on my nerves.'
The stack of music sheets has shrunk considerably, another 240 repeats.
'I'd say we'll be done in four hours', the production manager says.

2.12: Igor goes to the toilet, taking his phone with him. 'Someone's claiming on Twitter that I've miscounted, and I'm only playing 838 repetitions, oh God.'

2.18: The phrases become more fragmented, Igor is now isolating the notes; their connection isn't organic in any case, it's only asserted. The piece, which was a long quiet river at the beginning, disintegrating first into large pieces, then smaller fragments.

2.45: 'Are you still ok?' Igor asks the camera operators. 'I'll get a move on.'

Another 140. 'My head's slowly starting to swim.'

3.13: 'Sorry, people, I'm just taking ten minutes. I'd like to lie down here on the sofa for a bit.'
'All ok? Are you feeling all right?'
'Why are you asking? Does it sound like shit?'
Igor closes his eyes.

'I think I ate too much pineapple, I don't feel great.'
'That's possible', Olli says. 'Do you need something?'
'I'd love some chicken in breadcrumbs.'

On it goes, the next bits, the stack has almost disappeared. Igor speeds up again.

'How much longer do you need?' the production manager asks.
'Not that long. Why?'
'Then I'll cancel the last two technical shifts.'
'I'd love some chicken in breadcrumbs!'

3.51: The last 100.
'How many people are still here?'
'177,000 on YouTube.'
'Really?'
'No idea.'

'What would happen if I said at the end that as an encore I'd discovered a posthumous Satie piece with 1,440 repetitions?'
Outside it's slowly brightening; you can see the dawn through the toilet window.

The last thirty. Fortissimo, molto espressivo. Then from forte to a decrescendo, with a lot of pedal, down to nothing or hardly anything.

The last twenty.
Fifteen.
He takes the tempo out of the music, the notes now barely have body and contour, the melody sounds spherical and dreamy.

Igor looks into the camera, empty and exhausted, then straight ahead again. Drinks. Yawns. Drinks.

In the stack in front of him there can be no more than five sheets.

Plays another repetition.
One more.
One more.
And one more.
Throws the sheet on the floor, it should have been the second-last one, it's hard to tell from outside of the room.
Plays.
It's 5.12.
Plays.
No, it wasn't the second-last one.
Plays another repetition.
Checks the last sheet to see if it really is the last one.
The music has no tempo now.
Everything's in shreds, nothing left but scraps.
5.27: The theme for the last time.
The notes fade away.
5.28: It's over.
Igor breathes and closes the lid over the keys.
Gets to his feet. And goes.

And immediately he's in a good mood again. 'Thank you! That was great. Let's do it again next week.'

'So, now the second movement.'

'Shit. Forgot the music.'

Kristin Schuster calls and he asks her, laughing: 'Ok, so what's next?'

While the camera operators and the rest of the team gradually start dismantling everything, Igor walks over to the piano and plays a few bars from Richard Wagner's opera *Götterdämmerung*. Someone opens the big grand-piano door, the birds are singing outside, the morning air streams in. Everybody's completely exhausted. Igor's in a dazzling mood.

'So, after two or three hours or so I really stopped enjoying it. But now I could do it all over again. What are we going to do now?'

Olli drives Igor home; it's Whit Sunday, half past six in the morning, Berlin seems deserted, and they almost jump a red light.

In his apartment Igor puts on some coffee and serves slices of bread with liverwurst, then googles 'world's longest piano pieces', and nobody speaks.

If he wanted, Igor could make himself quite rich with *Vexations*. He would have to play them twice a year in a Berlin art gallery, as a performance piece. Or not? 'Do it yourself. Come on, I'm really not interested.'

Then he walks over to the piano and comes back with some sheet music. Twenty-four Preludes and Fugues by Wsewolod Zaderadski. 'This is,' Igor says, 'really a jewel of the millennium.

Zaderadski wrote the pieces in the gulag, on whatever happened to be around, because there was no manuscript paper. 'You hear that and you think, this is a composer ripping off Shostakovich. But the fact is that the pieces are 20 years older than the Shostakovich ones. No dynamics, no playing instructions, nothing. Incredibly brilliant music, but really hard. And some of the pieces sound like the music from old Soviet cartoons. Here, listen to this.' He goes to the piano and plays a Zaderadski fugue, then he takes his phone out of his pocket and searches YouTube for an episode of the Russian children's series *Cheburashka*. 'There, you hear that?' Definitely. 'It's so, so moving!' The song is one of the ones on which Igor once accompanied himself on the piano.

'So, what now?'
'Sleep!'
'I can't.'

At midday Igor posts a video of his hands, still playing *Vexations* on a garden table. The caption to the picture: repetition 1217.

#

His friend Felix Broede has taken the photographs for his CD covers from the beginning. The story of how they met is a fine example of how Igor meets the people that he works with. Almost all of them entered Igor's life by chance, but there's nothing random about their collaboration – that's based on the fact that Igor wants it.

'You might remember, in 2008 there was this huge story where the Beethoven House in Bonn collected money to buy the original manuscript of the Diabelli Variations. At the time the *Kulturzeit* programme showed different pianists playing the variations – Felix made that. He called Gerrit Glaner at Steinway and said: I need someone who's good but not famous. Gerrit had heard me at the Rubinstein Competition in Tel Aviv. So I met Felix, and on that first day we talked for five hours.'

This mode of collaboration tells you a lot about Igor. He would have every right to get involved in every detail, to control everything; a lot of artists do that. But he prefers to rely on a photographer knowing more about making pictures than he does.

'I really don't want to see the photographs that Felix takes. I tell him: I trust you, take our photographs, I know you know what you're doing – you decide which ones are good and which aren't. That's how it is at concerts when the technical guys ask me how I would like to have the light on the stage. Just do it, you know best what's going to look good. If the piano tuner asks me what I would like before a concert, I often don't know what to say. Or my hairdresser – he's learned to cut hair, I haven't. He's been doing it for years; why would he ask me?'

This mode of complete trust gives Igor the freedom to concentrate on other themes of his own. But the main reason for it is a different one: the joy at having people around him that he can trust. They are essential for his work; he stresses that over and over again. It's a relief to him to know he has other people around him. And: it eases his self-doubts.

'I still have the feeling that really I can't do it. I'm not good enough. There are reasons why I want a partner for many of my projects.'

Who he trusts and who he doesn't is not based on rational criteria: it's a lot more complicated: a gut feeling. Anyone who has his trust can be sure that it won't disappear again too quickly. But anyone who has it taken away will find it hard to get back.

'He's rigorous in some respects', says his friend Simon Bode. 'Of course that's also part of his recipe for success, that he simply parts company from people who have disappointed him, or who don't work as he needs them to. He isn't nostalgic.'

#

A week after *Vexations* Igor gives a concert in Vienna.

The events were planned a long time in advance. After his return from the USA, Igor was due to play Beethoven's Piano Concerto No. 5, followed on one evening by Beethoven's Third, and on the second evening by the Seventh Symphony. Good dates from the perspective at the time, good to shine but not extraordinary.

Now that's exactly what they are.

They're the first concerts in Vienna after a break of 88 days. When the artistic director steps up to the podium to greet the audience, he has a frantic reception; then he immediately makes it clear how he sees the magnitude of the event: the Konzerthaus has been closed only three times in its history. Once for ten days in February 1934 because of civil war. Then for 26 days in April 1945, because of a world war. And now for 88 days, a long time, 'emotionally and also economically', the artistic director says.

Vienna looked as if it had died, and only the tourists were missing – the day before, travel regulations were loosened to the extent that it was even possible to enter the country from Germany without having to demonstrate a Covid test. The airport was still in crisis mode; on the way to the luggage carousels Austrian soldiers stood taking temperatures, and in the spectrally empty lobby an automated female voice was ordering everyone to go home immediately and avoid social contact as much as possible. Many restaurants in the city centre had closed, and the sausage sellers gazed out sadly from their stalls.

The concert was due to happen not in the main auditorium of the Konzerthaus, but in the considerably smaller Mozart-Saal. An audience of 100 was allowed, placed individually in groups of two, three and four. The concert hall has a capacity of almost 700, and 600 seats were empty. The ushers asked everybody not to stand up after taking their seats. The orchestra came onto the podium not at the start of the concert, but one musician at a time, staggered over fifteen minutes. When everyone was seated, there were only a few fewer people on the podium than in the auditorium. The programme had also been changed: because the event was only supposed to last an hour, intervals were not allowed. Igor played not Beethoven, but Mozart's Piano Concerto No. 12, half the length and much less striking; otherwise, this concert needed fewer brass instruments in the orchestra, which minimized both expense and the danger of infection. After that the orchestra played a suite by Edvard Grieg. And then: the whole concert all over again, in front of a hundred new audience members.

Igor plays as if it's perfectly normal.
And while he is playing, it is all perfectly normal.
Igor at the piano, with the orchestra around him, and the natural order is re-established. For today.

Rather than shaking the concertmaster's hand, the pair rub elbows. During the orchestral exposition Igor blinks into the audience with anticipation and a degree of disbelief. The orchestra has a very rich sound; the musicians have also been looking forward to the day, and it takes them a while to get the balance right. It has never mattered less than it does today.

Igor pounces on the music like a starving man. He takes every phrase, every note as seriously as if he had decided not to show that the innocent skirmish of notes isn't really making huge demands on him. As if to establish that this programme is not a second choice, a compromise made in the context of the current situation.
As if it was exactly what he had planned.
Music is music.
And excuse me, we're talking about Mozart in Vienna.

After the first concert, Igor welcomes some well-wishers into the green room, gives first an interview for television, then another for radio, after which he opens the window, turns around and says with a grin, 'Sounds ok, doesn't it?'

Then he slumps into a plush-covered armchair. His suitcase was lost when he was changing flights in Frankfurt, and that morning he had to get hold of two T-shirts from a gentlemen's outfitters that he knows. 'I told him straight away, give me the ones for 40 euros, not the ones for 400, and then all of a sudden he also brings me two pairs of trousers, a jacket and shoes, so yeah. Now, yet again, I've spent half my fee for the evening.'

He shuts the window again before sitting down, and starts whispering.
'It's quite different from before! Quite different!'
Really?
'Yep! And you know why? Because I notice that there's so much that I really don't care about. Whether there are a

thousand people sitting there or two. Whether people are alert and attentive, or whether they're dozing away in their seats. How I'm dressed. Whether I really wait 30 seconds by the stage door before my performance, or not. All this ...' he tugs at his trousers and his shirt – 'I don't want any of it any more. I don't care about it any more.'

He falls silent and looks triumphant.

'The pressure's gone, do you see that? Gone! And I don't want it to come back.'

Pressure? Hasn't he always claimed there's no pressure for him, and that the stage and everyday life are one and the same?

'Yes, that's what I thought too. I'm noticing right now that it's not true. Now I care even less about it than I did before.'

He draws his left leg up under his backside.

'I want it to be like the house concerts. I want it to stay that way. I just want to do my thing and play.'

Then he says he's been thinking of playing 'Amazing Grace' as an encore; a few days before a man was allegedly murdered because of the colour of his skin, and it's the weekend of the anti-racism demonstrations. 'But it doesn't sound good on the piano. Listen.' He looks on his phone for a YouTube video: Aretha Franklin, accompanied on acoustic and Fender pianos. 'You need this organ for the harmonies; it doesn't sound like anything on just the piano. Anyway, I can't play it, it would be cultural appropriation. And probably nobody would under-stand it.'

He looks at the clock near the door. 'Right. In a minute I've got to do the Mozart again', he says. 'I'm really worried.' And he grins.

People are being let into the concert hall and it all starts over again. It may be that the concert is the first one that's been possible, but right now it's becoming clear: it needn't mean anything. This concert isn't the rescue, the salvation, the light at the end of the tunnel, a return to everyday life, to normality. It would be a mistake to interpret all that into it. It would be easy to persuade oneself that everything's fine again just because you can play Mozart in front of a hundred people again. The concert is just a concert, after many weeks without, before more weeks without.

When the audience and the musicians have taken their seats, the artistic director speaks again. Again: applause, again 1934, 1945, 2020. Then, again, Igor.

As an encore he plays the waltz from Dance of the Dolls by Shostakovich, later the Moment Musical Opus 94 by Schubert, and the audience applauds as if it's been waiting for all this for 88 days.

As it has.

And as Igor has too.

Now at last he can get back to doing what he likes doing: working. But he's under no illusions. When the radio journalist asks him during the interval whether he's glad that things are getting back to normal, he replies: they really aren't.

He leaves the building during the second concert, while the orchestra is still playing.

#

He calls a few days later.

'Listen up, I've got a joke for you. Old Herr Grün is on a train. A woman sits down opposite him, says nothing, looks at him. After ten minutes she asks: Forgive me, can I just ask, are you a Jew?

I'm sorry, Grün says, no, I'm not.

After a few minutes the woman asks again: Tell me, are you really not a Jew?

I'm really not, says Grün.

A short time later the woman asks again. Are you really sure you aren't a Jew? Grün looks wearily at the woman: Ok then, fine, I'm a Jew, what about it?

Odd, the woman says, you don't look Jewish at all.'

That's one of the first things you learn about Igor if you spend a lot of time with him. He always wants to be taken seriously, always. He's even serious when he's telling jokes.

\#

Thursday, 25 June 2020, the morning in Berlin is cool. Igor rides his folding bike to Central Station, boards the train to Hamburg, then cycles to the Elbphilharmonie, entering the Large Hall four minutes before the rehearsal is due to start.

He's a soloist in the end-of-season concert of the NDR Elbphilharmonie Orchestra – the calendar end of a season that really ended months ago, in this very auditorium: with Igor's concert on 10 March. This concert feels more like a new start than a conclusion. The NDR Elbphilharmonie Orchestra sits on the podium in a very reduced version: twelve violins, four violas, three cellos, two double basses. Since mid-March there haven't been many events with nearly as many musicians.

Igor plays the piano part in the Concerto for Piano and Trumpet Opus 35 by Dmitri Shostakovich, a piece barely twenty minutes long, for long stretches less like a conventional piano concerto and more like a well-told joke, and Igor sits at the instrument in the pose of the joke-teller: looking as serious as possible. The piece is conducted by Alan Gilbert, chief conductor of the orchestra for this season, who has flown in from Stockholm for the rehearsals. Igor greets him with a fist raised in solidarity. Gilbert returns the gesture and off they go.

First movement, Allegretto, the runs ripple into the emptiness of the room, the melody begins, something goes wrong in the violins, from the top.

The lid has been unscrewed on the piano. It's not clear whether it's for acoustic reasons or because the lid would disturb the camera angle. The seats are empty: the audience for the concert will be sitting at home by the radio or in front of the television, and the rehearsal is also a rehearsal for the camera operators and the NDR team responsible for the livestream. At the rehearsal there are distinctly more camera operators and technicians in the auditorium than there are orchestral musicians on stage.

At the third attempt the beginning comes together. They play all the way through the first movement, and the camera crane sweeps once diagonally through the hall. 'That was great', Gilbert says, meaning the music; 'let's keep going'. In the second movement the violins don't sound quite together. Gilbert has them go through the passage again and again, then a voice from a speaker echoes through the hall: 'Camera three, careful, I'm coming in from the left.' For three seconds Gilbert and the others ignore the disturbance; then they break off.

'Quiet please', says someone from the orchestra.
'We have technical problems', says the head of recording.
'We noticed', Gilbert says.
'And heard', says Igor. He plays the tatata-taa from Beethoven's Fifth, the leader replies and a third musician joins in. Laughter.

Gilbert works on nuances with the orchestra; the long quiet tones in the violins still aren't quite together. Igor leaves the hall and goes to the toilet. 'Where is he?' Gilbert asks, then counts in and plays. Two seconds before his entry, Igor appears back at the piano.

There's noise from the technician's corner again, and the voice rings out from the speaker. Gilbert breaks off. 'We don't want to disturb you', he says with a hint of sarcasm. 'We're still having technical problems; unfortunately they might go on for another few minutes.' 'And now? Should we wait?' – 'I'm really sorry.' – Gilbert turns to the orchestra: 'In English we say, the tail wags the dog.'

The concert is the opposite of Levit's house concerts: an extreme technical outlay. For today, the camera crane alone costs a small fortune.

Gilbert goes on with the rehearsal; the second movement still isn't quite gelling. Switches of tempo, staccato, the unison strings are lying apart, Gilbert won't let go, he sings along, Igor grins and boxes the piano stool with his right first. He's getting bored, and peers at the camera crane.

Then the third movement, finally, all in one go, and into the fourth. At the end of the concert the trumpet takes over and the piano becomes the accompaniment, a virtuoso accompaniment admittedly, but still just an accompaniment, an interesting plot twist. Gilbert speeds up, the orchestra runs through the bars, 'fast enough?' Gilbert asks when they're finished. 'Yes', Igor says and picks up the water bottle, 'fast enough.'

From the top again, now making deliberately for the danger spots. Second movement, first violins. Igor plays, the violins come in, 'that one note', Gilbert says, 'is always late.' Starting again, the violins again, 'sorry to say, still too late', Gilbert says. To Igor. 'Do you want the trumpet passage from the end again?'

Igor: 'No, the way he plays it is wonderful.'

One last time.

A run-through for the camera crane.

No complications.

'Great, thank you!'

Igor waves and leaps off the stage. He has a meeting, lunch with the senator for culture.

The next evening, at the concert, the orchestra gets to its feet when Gilbert enters the auditorium with Igor, a ritual from a time when the audience was in the hall as well. Now, apart from the music critic of the *Hamburger Abendblatt*, there's nobody there.

In the interval discussion, recorded in the empty stairwell of the Elbphilharmonie, Igor and Alan Gilbert talk about the circumstances under which the concert is taking place.

Gilbert says he's only conducted it once, while Igor knows it inside out. An anarchic piece, Igor says. 'Are there rules? Let's break them. Is there certainty? Let's destroy it. It has its bleak passages, it's not cheerful, it's optimistic. It's progressive.'

'How long did it take us to decide on the Shostakovich concert?'

'Two weeks.'

'Isn't that wonderful?'

A few days after the concert Igor calls.

'You know what the best thing of all was? That concert felt like visiting a café. I leave the house, get on my folding bike, ride to the station, board the train to Hamburg, no luggage, just a little rucksack. I arrive in Hamburg, get back on my bike, ride to the concert hall, say "Moin" like they do there, rehearse for a few minutes, change my T-shirt, play, then I say "Tschüss", cycle back to the station and then home. It was so easy. The whole pressure-to-perform thing has completely gone. All those questions – what do I sound like, what am I going to wear, how many seconds will I spend waiting behind the stage door before my appearance – gone! I've always been relaxed about all those things, but there are still lots of things I need to think about. All that pressure has completely gone, the whole thing feels so much easier – and I really like that very much.

And that doesn't make the concert any less important.

I also very much liked the way we made sure there wasn't a deadly silence after the last note – we stood up, we applauded each other, mucked around a bit and left. What else are you going to do? Am I supposed to bow to the empty rows? It was so easy!

I really can't be bothered with that whole ritual any more; in fact I just want to do things like that. It feels so incredibly easy and beautiful right now. And as I say: I'm going to do everything I can to make sure it stays that way.

It's all down to me. I'm the one who thinks I need to move. Nobody's forcing me to. I'm the one who can say, now after Opus 111 I'm going to play a piece by Carlos Jobim. It's in my hands. I just have to do it. I just have to trust myself.'

#

At the beginning of July, Igor takes a trip to the mountains for a few days.

Hiking, cycling, breathing in the air. Another month till Salzburg. The concert business is slowly getting going again, on a lower level than before, but it's going. The audience sits in the concert hall with facial protection, a safe distance apart. In some venues a third of the seats are occupied when the house is sold out, in others a quarter. Almost all the organizers ask

Igor to shorten the programme, and to play the concert twice in the evening.

What's it going to be like in Salzburg?

'Something's going to happen. I'm not a difficult patient, I just need a piano on the stage. I find all these questions a bit tiring.'

Igor is just back from an extended bicycle tour; now he's sitting in his hotel room in his dressing gown, happy but tired. Our conversations when he is tired are always the best ones because then he has to make an effort to get over the tiredness.

'I have a feeling', Igor says, 'that I'm writing the last chapter of my life. I mean: I've played a whole lot of piano for very many years. I've learned a ridiculous number of pieces and given a very large number of concerts. Have we ever talked about Anthony Bourdain?'

The chef? Not a word.

'Ok, imagine I've been running a restaurant quite successfully for six years. I've got loads of customers, many of them keep coming back, I stand in the kitchen every day, I come up with menus, I'm always at it. I take it all very seriously, but by now I've also got the confidence that says to me: if I go on taking my work seriously and don't stop trying, then the show's going to keep going. I don't have to prove to anyone that the restaurant is ok. My guests trust me, I can develop new recipes, but the institution stays standing. And now? Now I'd like to do something new. I don't want to give up the restaurant, I still want to be in the kitchen and plan menus, but now there has to be something new as well. Do you get it?'

Not entirely.

'For me, playing the piano is the most beautiful thing of all. It's not hard for me, I can – with a few exceptions – learn any piece I want to. Now would be a good time to make myself superfluous in this business for a bit. The show's going to go on anyway, the quality is right, I'll keep turning up every now and again and standing by the stove myself, just not constantly.'

Yes, but isn't the difference that if you have an evening of piano music with Igor Levit, no one else can sit at the piano for you?

'Yes, of course, in the end I still have to be the one playing. But I'd like to have more content in my life than just the piano. My life as a concert pianist is working right now. It doesn't work all by itself, but it works. And the status quo doesn't interest me.'

What could that mean? What's next?

'I don't know yet, I haven't quite got there. I might start organizing concerts, inviting other musicians to join me, travelling – I have a whole lot of chaotic thoughts on the subject. But over the last few days I've come to realize: I don't want to go back to my pre-pandemic life.'

He gets up.

'So, my dear man. I'm going out now, I'm going up another small mountain.'

#

The next day Igor calls and the conversation turns to *Vexations*.

'I'd like to do that again. Seriously. It's the first time in my life that I've wanted to repeat something. That was really very,

very brilliant. I have very lovely memories of it; to be quite honest, I even miss that atmosphere a bit.

'The room, the people in it, all the trappings, the preparation, the result. Of course it was a physical strain to play it, and there were a few minutes when I felt I couldn't be bothered any more. But in retrospect I don't find it a strain at all; on the contrary, I look back on it with a feeling of great lightness.'

The Berlin auction house Grisebach has auctioned the sheets of music, bringing in 25,000 euros. Igor is donating the money to FREO, an association that represents independent ensembles and orchestras.

#

Saturday, 1 August 2020. Just a few weeks ago nobody had seriously expected that the Salzburg Festival would really happen. While the premiere is being held in the Grosses Festspielhaus, Igor is sitting sockless in Birkenstocks and reading outside the Blaue Gans restaurant. The signal is clear: this is where he's at home.

The next day he's playing the Waldstein Sonata, and the music sounds as if it's aged by a year.

Why does he particularly like playing the Beethoven sonatas?

'Those pieces are unending challenges: technically, pianistically, musically. One day I think, I know the piece now, I've understood it now, I can play it now. And a day later it's completely gone. That's the dangerous thing – and the inspiring one, because it never gets boring. It never stops.'

The sonatas are very meticulously worked out. Almost every single note is given its own playing instruction. And then there are the extreme dynamic leaps – Beethoven is a stranger to the middle way.

'There is piano, there is forte, pianissimo, fortissimo, I think I know three or four mezzoforte or mezzopiano moments in the whole of his piano works. All of that indicates an enormous self-confidence, an understanding of what he wanted. The difficulty often lies in the fact that contrasting things are happening in very quick succession in a very narrow space. That's exactly what I enjoy. And anyone who plays it can feel strengthened, not by serving the music, but by saying: I'm here, I matter, look at what this music is doing to me.'

In an interview Igor was asked how often he had to play the sonatas until he was sure about them. 'Before I recorded them, maybe twenty or thirty times', was Igor's answer. 'Played at home: maybe ten thousand times. Played, read, heard, thought: fifty thousand times.'

\#

When Igor's favourite café chain opened a branch in the summer of 2011, Igor met the Hanover artist Hannes Malte Mahler.

'I had already heard of him. Somebody told me he made very good business cards. At the time I thought I needed business cards, so I approached him, saying: "You are Hannes Malte Mahler, you're the business card guy." He got incredibly angry. "How dare you, business card guy – I'm a qualified artist, everything I do is art!" We immediately got on very well and arranged to meet for breakfast the next day.'

Igor was 24, Mahler was 43, and they immediately hit it off.

'From that day onwards, we saw each other almost every day when I was in Hanover. He was inspiring, very lively and very intelligent; he had lots of ideas – and he had lived, he was a real bon viveur, and a total beau. He walked through the area in green socks and a tank top, and 20 minutes later he would be sitting with the Rotarians, suited up and smoking a cigar. He could play with situations, he knew how to present himself, but he was never ridiculous, always very much in control. He had no idea about classical music, and he was wild about it. He was a person who was always there for me. There was barely a moment when he would have said: sorry, no time.'

Mahler made his money as an advertising executive, photographer and web designer; worked as a hospital orderly; and bred pigs. Igor says he was the most important person to him outside of his family.

When Igor first played the Hammerklavier Sonata in concert at the Brandenburg Music Festival in Finsterwalde, Mahler drove him to the concert hall in his red Mercedes, and before the performance they had a three-euro kebab from a stall.

Once Igor complained to him about the fugue in the Hammerklavier Sonata. He said: play some other thing in B flat major, nobody will notice.

When Igor had his debut in the Berlin Philharmonie, Mahler waited backstage for him to go on. 'I was wearing a dinner jacket for the first time in my life and had no idea how to do up a bow tie. I don't think he did either. We stood there, I didn't really care about the performance, but I knew I couldn't go out there without a bow tie, and he stood there and tied it around my neck – and I don't know how, but he managed. He was incredibly proud of it, and he was also incredibly proud of me.'

Mahler was there when Igor discussed the design of the first album with the record company. 'He was my pit bull. The conversation went brilliantly, we all reached a quick agreement, and at the crucial moment I just had to look at him and ask: do you like it too? He just said "Yes" and nothing more. But I knew he was there. I don't like doing my things on my own, and there are reasons for that.'

Mahler consoled Igor on the day his debut CD was released, when the woman he now calls his first great love left him. 'I read her message, then I called him. I was standing in the concert hall in Copenhagen, and was due to play the Beethoven Piano Concerto No. 5, with Fabio Luisi. The green room opens up directly onto the canal. When Mahler picked up, I told him what she had written, and then said: now you have exactly one choice, either you say something right or I throw myself in the canal. I can't remember what he said, but it must have been the right thing – I lay down on the floor and stayed down there for a long time. Then I went downstairs and played Beethoven.'

Mahler flew to join Igor when he played the Goldberg Variations in New York with Marina Abramovic.

When Igor played 'The People United Will Never Be Defeated!' at the KunstFestSpiele in Herrenhausen in 2013, Frederic Rzewski was sitting next to Mahler in the audience. Igor introduced them to one another.

Later Igor and Rzewski shared a recital in Hanover. Igor played 'People United', Rzewski the Hammerklavier Sonata.

As an encore Rzewski played his composition 'A Mensch'. In his introduction he explained: "'A Mensch" is Yiddish and means "good person", a Mensch is a person of honour.'

'I got all that from Rzewski', Igor says.

He played the encore in memory of a friend, Rzewski says.

In 2016 Igor played the piece in memory of Mahler.

'I hadn't had a friendship like that until then, that much is clear. It could be that there was a void in my life that he filled – an unconscious one, undoubtedly. I've never had a connection with anyone in my life like the one I had with Mahler. And when he died, I had the first real breakdown in my life. After that day nothing for me was the way it was before. To be honest I don't remember what I was like before. And I'm not interested in it.'

At their concert in Ludwigsburg two days later, Igor asked Simon to sing Mahler's favourite song, 'Frisch gesungen', as an encore.

'I played, Simon started singing, and two bars later I thought, I'm stopping, because I couldn't do it, and at that moment a small miracle happened. I had just announced why we were playing that song – and just at the moment when I couldn't go on, the people in the auditorium started singing along. I've never experienced anything like it. I'm really not a superstitious person – but at that moment I had the feeling that somebody up there had raised the conductor's baton and said: right, now help him or it's over.'

Mahler made the painting that can be seen on Igor's living room wall in the first house concerts: 'Gladiolus', a big blossom floating above an estate of terraced houses. Igor still has a second painting by the artist: a little helicopter rising into the air. The title: 'Peter Pan or Why Men Never Grow Up'.

'Now, four years after his death, there's no longer a gaping hole in my life', Igor says, 'but there's a great longing for that feeling of being able to be completely oneself in the presence of another person.'

\#

A rainy day in Salzburg; brown water laps the rim of the Salzach embankment, and we meet for a late breakfast in the Blaue Gans. Igor drinks camomile tea; he's got an upset stomach and he's feeling tense.

A good moment for a very basic, very bold question.
What do you actually stand for politically?
The answer comes in a flash.

'That's a really bold question.'

He takes a sip of tea.

'That's actually too bold for me.'

Then he answers anyway.

'I stand for not flushing this planet down the toilet, which is what we're doing right now. I stand for not letting people drown in the sea as if they were second-class people.

I stand for not working towards an economic system that is based ultimately on the destruction of the planet and of the economic opportunities of countless people.

I stand for finally acknowledging that our affluence and many other things that we consider normal have grown at the expense of other people. Those other people have a voice in social media, and can communicate, unlike before. We should listen to them, learn from them and give them their share. I'm absolutely sure we're going to have to surrender some space. There are studies into the climate crisis that say: a significant component of the fight against the crisis means reducing our living space. Not everyone can do that; a lot of people already have too little room, but others have too much. So let's go, what are we waiting for?

I stand for participation, for giving something up in order to let other people have a share, to let them live. No one in the world needs to be a billionaire.

I stand for the conviction that too much power in the hands of too many people is really dangerous.

I also stand for acknowledging that the days are gone when an older generation says to a younger one: now wait till it's your turn. That's over, and I'm glad.

Also: I wish there could be a debate again. When someone writes an article on a subject, any subject, and you find 30 per cent of the arguments bearable and 70 per cent not: then write against it, answer, give counter-arguments! But don't take a screenshot of individual sentences and get worked up about them on Twitter – that's not an argument, that's crazy.

And I'm rigorously opposed to falling into self-censorship. I find self-censorship extremely dangerous. I have colleagues, and I include myself in this, who are very careful what they say about China – they know if they say anything they'll never perform there again, so they prefer not to express themselves.

I stand for the freedom to call a spade a spade, to name people by name if there's a reason for it – and without fear. I don't always manage to do that myself, but I try.

Once in New York a patron of the arts came up to me and criticized my tweets against Trump, which he couldn't stand. I think I gave him quite a decent reply. I asked: isn't that exactly the kind of individualism that you're fighting for all day? You have your opinion, I have mine, and we're standing here together: isn't that exactly what you want? Then he grinned and said: Yep. That's what it's about. I think his position's wrong, he thinks mine's wrong, but we can still stand face to face and talk. I was a bit proud of myself.

In my working life nobody's ever held who I am against me. Never. I don't even think about that. And to be honest: I just stand for curiosity. For openness. For change. Anything that doesn't change dies. I quite firmly believe that.'

#

A few days later, on the day of the Appassionata, Igor has spent the morning at the piano in the Mozart-Saal. The sun is shining again, we meet up for lunch – and the theme of politics isn't quite done.

Because there are two points in Igor's thought that plainly contradict one another.

One concerns the tone of his criticism of far-right politicians: how does he reconcile his assertion that there are no second-class people with his attitude towards politicians he disagrees with?

In concrete terms: what answer can he give to *BILD* journalists who tell him he can't argue against hate speech on the net and at the same time say that an AfD politician has shed his humanity?

'The point is: people are never interested in how things are, but only in what they think about it. I said he'd forfeited his humanity; I explained what I meant by that. Then a few people twisted my words and claimed I'd denied human dignity to all AfD voters – but I hadn't done that, and anyone who claims I did is lying. It's a distortion of the facts, and also a favourite trick of right-wing populists. I was speaking about a single very concrete moment, in which an AfD functionary spread the lie, in front of the cameras, that a male refugee had raped a girl, in a politically very heated situation.

But nobody talks about that. Everybody talks about how they found what Igor Levit tweeted about it. It's not about the thing itself, but about sensibilities. That happens often: someone proposes a topic, wants to talk about anti-Semitism, but rather than talking about anti-Semitism they talk about the issue of whether the author himself has always done the right thing. In that way a lot of big topics are systematically made small – and that bothers me a lot. And the same thing was true in this case: a politician stirs up resentments with a lie, but the rage is fuelled by the fact that I tweeted something that two Springer journalists didn't like. That's grotesque. And to that extent I don't see a contradiction. I stand by what I said; I have nothing to add and nothing to take away.'

The waiter stands beside the table, and we order: corn-fed chicken with grilled vegetables, 'shame it isn't vegetarian', Igor says.

The second contradiction: if he's so vehemently in favour of climate protection, how does he reconcile that with having to fly – at least before the pandemic – from concert to concert as a pianist?

'Yes, that is a contradiction', Igor says. 'There's no denying it; I've lived with that contradiction since I've been performing. Now, with Covid, I find flying revolting. The planes are full, it's airless, nobody keeps their distance, I find it really unpleasant. I only fly if there's really no other option. Sure, for reasons other than climate protection, but that's how it is. I don't want to make myself sound more innocent than I am. And apart from that: only very dangerous people believe in an absolute lack of contradiction.

But for me climate protection has nothing to do with making yourself a hero. If I decide I'm not flying any more, that decision makes a difference – although a small one. Climate politics would mean that this decision has already been made for everybody, with a much, much, much greater effect. But unfortunately that hardly ever happens.'

\#

One more quick question: can music on its own save anything?

– No.

– Can music save something for you when you play it?

– I don't know.

– Are you interested in that? Can attitudes be changed, opinions turned around, ideas formed with music?

– No, they can't. The fascists sitting there in parliament will also happily go to the theatre and the opera. That's always been the case. Nothing can be turned around like that. Music doesn't make laws, it's still us human beings who do that.

#

Then Igor plays the Appassionata. The concert begins at 5.00 pm, the audience are sitting masked in the concert hall.

Igor plunges into the music. He arranges the world and at the same time fundamentally calls it into question, despairs of it, rescues it just before it perishes.

The people in the concert hall listen raptly.

'I'm the middle of the world for those one and a half, two hours', Igor once said of himself. 'The people in the audience all have to be quiet, if you please, and listen to me, how I'm doing, it, what I'm trying to do. And I get paid for it. It sounds insanely egocentric. And at the moment it is. I'm the centre of the world. In the end, what am I doing, what's my task? I go out to arouse emotions in people. That means I surrender something, something of myself. I turn my inside outwards. And I'm fully convinced that how you are is also how you play.'

And while he plays and plays, it becomes increasingly clear what makes him so special as a pianist. His status as an exceptional talent is limited to the piano stool. Away from it he is a quite normal person; he doesn't present himself as the genius of the century, he doesn't have the manners of the great artist who lives only for music, in a world in which the most important laws are related to dominant seventh chords and suspended fourths, but in the same world as his audience.

And the result of that is that when he plays you don't have the feeling that you're turning away from reality and towards art.

He says things that anyone else could say.

The observations that his devotees celebrate as political statements aren't particularly complex; they're quite simple thoughts that any other person could have had.

He shows what would also be possible for any other person.

Anybody could do that.

It's even stating the obvious.

The fact that Igor stands out only shows that so many people aren't doing that.

Away from the piano he's no better than the rest of us.

Or perhaps there's a better way of putting it: he's exactly as good as any of us could be.

#

In 2018, when the rappers Kollegah and Farid Bang received an ECHO award for an album with lyrics that could have been read as mocking concentration camp victims, Igor gave back the award that he had received in 2014 for his debut CD.

When the ECHO was abolished a short time afterwards, and the ECHO Klassik was replaced with the Opus Klassik, Igor called that decision cowardly in a TV interview:

'Because those responsible – rather than facing up to it, rather than saying: yes, we fucked up here, and rather than apologizing – rather than facing up to it as an association that deals with culture, and saying: yes, we haven't done any favours to issues about racism in society, about anti-Semitism, about homophobia, about misogyny, to put it kindly. Now we're going to face up to things, we're going to face up to the debate and assume responsibility, accept actual conse-quences – rather than doing that, both verbally and in their actions, they just say: ECHO is damaged as a brand, so let's do something new. That's really sad.'

Is it a political act when an artist gives back a prize because two rappers who have also received the prize say in one of their works that their bodies are 'more defined than those of Auschwitz inmates'?

For Igor the question doesn't arise, his instinct gives him the answer, and his instinct says: who cares about the question; to act otherwise would be disgraceful.

But it would be a mistake to imagine that Igor acts that way because he thinks the action is original. In this context originality isn't a relevant category. Quite the contrary.

For Igor, acting as he does is the exact opposite of original. It's obvious.

And he doesn't act as he does *even though* it's obvious, but *because* it is.

In October 2019 Igor was awarded the Opus Klassik for the album *Life.* Igor really didn't want to show up at the gala to accept the award, but his label insisted. Igor agreed on condition that he would be able to say something. A week before the gala a far-right attacker in Halle tried unsuccessfully to force his way into the synagogue, and then shot two innocent bystanders.

Once again, Igor jotted down his speech on a piece of paper.

'Ladies and gentlemen. Two years ago the ECHO fell apart. The reason for that was simple and the result inevitable. At the time we all lamented the coarsening of our language.

Today, two years later, after Halle, we are mourning two dead. Once again. And although some politicians speak of alarm signals and the helplessness of our reaction to this drama leaves us speechless, none of it is a surprise. After NSU [the National Socialist Underground, uncovered in 2011, responsible for a series of bank robberies, bombings and murders of immigrants], after countless attacks on mosques, synagogues, Jewish cemeteries, refugee hostels and so on, what's happening here is not a surprise. The attacks that are happening against all of us are all flourishing in the soil of coarsening language. It is language that can fatally poison societies. And no stage in this country should give room to this language, no parliamentary or legal space, and certainly no cultural space.

'We all bear responsibility, all of us together. Each and every one of us. For this country, which is home to us all. I dedicate my prize to all those who fight, quietly or loudly, against anti-Semitism, against islamophobia and against anti-feminism. All of these concepts have one thing in common: an absolute contempt for humanity. And last of all I also dedicate this prize to Jana L. and Kevin S. Their lives were taken in Halle. Pointlessly. And I also dedicate this prize to their memory.'

#

After his return from Salzburg Igor considered leaving Berlin. 'I have the feeling that this episode is coming to an end.'

We are sitting in Hamburg, on the terrace of a restaurant opposite the Elbphilharmonie. That morning Igor gave an interview to NDR television, along with Hamburg's senator for culture. It's the restaurant where Igor celebrated his birthday on 10 March after the last concert performed to a full house. Now he sees the concert hall looming in front of him, the sky reflected in its mirrored façade.

'When I came to Berlin, I wanted something different from today.'

What then?

'I wanted to go to Mitte, to the centre; I deliberately looked for an apartment near Soho House. I had different friends then, I had a different perspective on my life, things were going in a different direction. A lot has happened since that time, and a whole lot has changed.'

In 2014 Igor considered leaving Germany and going to New York, or perhaps somewhere else.

'Nothing came of it, for various reasons, and in the end I chickened out. It would have been pretty tough, and I wasn't up to it at the time. But the thought was there.'

He didn't let anybody in on his thoughts, which he immediately abandoned when his mother fell ill.

Then two years passed. And then it was Berlin.

'Everyone was going to Berlin in those days; the city struck me as a good compromise: a new city but one where I wouldn't be completely alone. My best friend Hannes was always in Berlin because his girlfriend at the time lived there. Georg too. Maxim and Maren lived in the city. The fact is, though: since coming home again I haven't felt right. I was never as tired as I have been since May. Tiredness is a pain, I can't sleep, it's really such a colossal pain.'

You can see in his face that that isn't all.

'And it also has something to do with the fact that – partly through my own fault, partly not – I've been alone for four and a half years. We've had this issue a few times where I've said: things acquire a meaning for me when I share them. And when I'm sitting in my apartment right now, I'm annoyed that I have it all to myself. It isn't the apartment's fault, the apartment is fantastic. I live on a wonderful street; it's all great. I just have the feeling that this chapter is slowly coming to a natural end. When that will be, in a year, in six months, two years, I can't yet say. And I don't know which chapter comes after that.'

#

In November 2011 Igor played a matinee in the Prinzregententheater in Munich: in the first half, parts of his D minor programme – a passacaglia by Johann Caspar Kerll, Beethoven's Tempest Sonata, Bach's D minor Chaconne in the version for left hand by Johannes Brahms, in the second half two pieces from the *Années de Pélerinage* by Franz Liszt.

Two days later a review appeared in the arts page of the *Süddeutsche Zeitung*. The author was unimpressed. Igor hadn't been able to demonstrate, with his playing, why the rarely performed Kerll Passacaglia absolutely deserved to be part of the current repertoire. For the much better-known Tempest Sonata, which demanded a more creative response from the pianist to the notes on the page, while he clearly wanted to do more than many other quite decent musicians, the vision that he had developed was 'not so much dramatically and classically valid as highly personal'. His tempi in particular still seemed to be in the experimental phase: often, after three notes, you didn't know where you were coming from and where it was going to go. Instead of a robust flow, dreamy islands formed, orphaned single notes that couldn't find their way to each other. In the four pieces from Liszt's *Années de Pélerinage*, what was more, Levit had lost himself again in 'slackly contourless, pallid dream landscapes'.

The hatchet job hit Igor hard.

Three years later the same author wrote of the Bach partita album that these pieces had not been written to be performed in the well-mannered, nondescript and lustreless way in which Levit reels off the partitas. Igor was in search of greatness, 'and it is simply exhausting to accompany him on this predictably very long journey.'

Further articles with a similar tone followed. Igor lacked a controlled lightness, which might also be explained by his playing technique: 'The extremes, the violence and the unrestrained use of the pedal obscure some rather distinctive mood-patterns, construct backdrops and simply render the other things unimportant.' Igor Levit's fundamental problem: that his reinterpretations sometimes sound like misunderstandings.

This writer was not alone. Another wrote about a matinee in the Prinzregententheater in November 2014 and further sharpened his critique: one could certainly talk about Igor's artistic attitude, 'if one did not so clearly sense the calculation behind it. Not a single note in this matinee sounded spontaneous, everything seemed to have been put in place in advance. Here is a young pianist obviously playing the great repertoire chiefly in order to put his own sensibility on display. And what triumphs is sadly not spirit, but its little brother: esoteric kitsch.'

Igor responded to the articles as anyone would have done. He was hurt, thrown and unsettled. Music criticism – like all art criticism – is an extremely subjective business, and apart from a demonstrable basis in fact, all judgements and criteria are only partially verifiable, the notes of the performance under discussion faded away long ago, and the object of examination is irrevocably lost.

This makes music criticism particularly demanding: if it's successful, it can be the deathless echo of the concert, a lasting footprint.

For musicians, the importance of reviews is different according to the different stages of their working lives. At the start of a career, a few positive lines can open some doors, and later on a poor review can have a much more dramatic effect on sales figures. In the end, at all stages of a career, there remains a constant fear of reading a newspaper article that strips the artist of their music and says, in different tones of voice: this really isn't as great as you might have thought.

'That first article hit home', Igor says. 'When you read the first big hatchet jobs on yourself in a national newspaper you don't find it especially funny – at first I really had no experience of the field whatsoever. A few authors have tried to disparage me for years at every opportunity – even in articles about concerts I didn't even play. That taught me to see things differently.'

After the first negative reviews Igor was miserable for days. He couldn't let go of them; he felt disappointed, both by the author of the article and by himself: as if what he was trying to express was not well enough formulated and had therefore been made ridiculous.

When Maren Borchers noticed how preoccupied he was, she said: if it's really a problem, you need to work on your confidence. It's not right that this is leaving you so downcast. You've got to shake it off. It's going to happen again and again. Get used to it.

The conversation repeated itself over several years with each new bad review. Igor grew through it; the articles still annoyed him but didn't bring him down any more. Maren Borchers says: they helped him grow up.

'The learning process was extremely unpleasant', Igor says. 'Unpleasant but very, very important, because you need go through something like that. I don't pretend not to read it. I read all the things that are written about me, and I'm really interested in them. But learning to keep them in perspective – that took some time. If someone thinks I'm playing badly, and he has nothing better to do than write an article about it, and a newspaper has nothing better to print, then it's their absolute right.'

But there is one accusation that he can't ignore: that he only acts out his emotions on stage, that he acts in a calculated rather than a spontaneous way. That's he's only pretending.

That opens up the old wound.

One of the critics on the *Süddeutsche Zeitung*, Helmut Mauró, repeated the accusation after a Beethoven matinee in Munich in 2018.

Igor Levit, he wrote, adhered strictly to Beethoven's instructions, as if to shield himself from any interpretational randomness. But sticking to the rules didn't make music, 'or only of a very brittle, bleak kind. It's a bit like acting: whether you can deliver the lines correctly, or act the part – in music, too, those are almost two different worlds.' Beethoven put the excitement in the sonatas; it's in the atoms of the melody and the molecules of the sounds. When Levit plays (the article continues), none of that is apparent, and even the most exciting passages sound lame and empty. 'And how is one supposed to play *ermattet* (exhaustedly), as it says on the sheet music, if there was barely any excitement beforehand?' the author writes, before answering his own question: the effect must be simulated.

A musician who only mimics emotional impulses because he hasn't grasped the true content of his art: both an original accusation and a cunning one. Hard to refute, but that's the least of the problems. One much greater one is the context out of which the accusation arises: it is the essay 'Das Judenthum in der Musik' (Jewishness in Music), in which Richard Wagner accuses non-German, and in particular Jewish, artists of not being capable of their own creation because of a lack of German spirit, and hence only ever imitating genuine art. A narrative eagerly cited by the National Socialists.

That Mauró, a musicologist, might be unfamiliar with the essay, and in Wagner's city of Munich to boot, is highly unlikely. Whether or not the critic from the *Süddeutsche Zeitung* deliberately intended the allusion: the idea at the heart of his criticism lies in a tainted anti-Semitic tradition.

And that with this gesture a German critic is telling Igor, the Jewish pianist, who and what he is, and who he needs to be: he doesn't get away with that one so easily.

So far.

Igor has grown through these attacks. 'He was always the one who said: don't read that, just ignore it', his mother says. 'I don't know if it's what he really felt. But he was able to distance himself. And if bad things like that were written about other people, he gave those people a lot of support.'

'But we must also be grateful to Mauró', his mother says. 'He made a lot of people aware of Igor. Since he started writing about Igor, the concerts in Munich have been sold out.'

\#

'I can't do poses', Igor says. 'I'm very good at tactics and planning; I've got a very good feeling for what to do and say when, and who I should work with. But I'm not putting on an act for anybody.'

That doesn't just apply to his concerts; it also applies to him as a public figure.
Igor Levit, the politically committed pianist of the century.

It's easy to misunderstand Igor as a very well-made, stage-managed, self-made artist figure. 'But that's not how it is', Maren Borchers says. 'That's not what he is. And I think that's also the secret to why there are so many people who follow him so unquestioningly. The public isn't stupid, and it only lets itself to be led by the nose to a certain extent. All these manufactured stars, marketing concepts – their half-life is worryingly short. And Igor isn't a manufactured star; people sense that. He's authentic.

'Because he just is how he is. He's vain, he's often angry and sometimes naïve, but it's all authentic.'

And that's how he stops people being afraid of music. That's what Igor always gets reflected back at him, above all during the house concerts. People who say: I don't know anything about classical music, and it's not something I'm interested in – but this touches me. And in the end, I don't have the feeling that I have to dress up smartly and have an idea about it. I don't even need to have much money to be able to buy concert tickets – I just listen. And what I feel when I'm listening has its justification.

\#

The question that remains open is the same one that was open at the beginning: where do things go from here?

Igor still hasn't got an answer.

'I have a relaxed, almost entirely disinterested relationship to all that talk. I hate talking about my career, I just don't want to.'

The danger that exists, the one that everyone's afraid of: that Igor might mess up, even though that has never happened so far. That his technique will suffer, even if it's been unscathed so far. That he'll forget about playing the piano by tweeting so much. Everybody knows: he can only live the life he's living as long as he keeps on playing piano at this level.

'With all the noise that we have going on around us right now, I also have to keep reminding people what it's actually all about', Igor's manager Kristin Schuster says.

Classical music is a market in which reliability counts. The most successful performers will be those who can be counted on to deliver more than they have promised.

In Igor's case that promise is getting bigger and bigger.
So far it's a promise that he's always kept.

'I remember', Simon Bode says, 'one time we were sitting in an old apartment in Berlin and he was questioning everything. Why do I make life so hard for myself? I'd also like to tour the whole world with only one piano concerto and get rich with it, so why don't I actually do that? And then I said: you'll have to discuss that with your people – if that's what you want, then do it. That happens a lot: those moments when he thinks, why am I making things so hard for myself – and then he remembers why. The huge repertoire, all those programmes:

that's what he wants. It's more that people advise him against it, and that he and his manager have to agree the programmes with the organizers. Everything that later becomes standard is hard at first because for a long time nobody wants it.'

At the moment Igor and Kristin are planning three years ahead, sometimes four.

'Igor wanted to do less, but I think now he knows how bad it is not playing concerts, he'll probably want to start doing it again', Kristin Schuster says. 'That depends on how the whole business changes. Nobody can predict that.'

Igor's desire is freedom. That means not having to draw up programmes three years in advance. Finding ways to give him the greatest possible freedom in which he can work – without making work impossible for all other partners. 'Since the arrival of Covid, if not before, nothing seems to be fixed in place. Now we have the biggest opportunity to do things differently, and maybe even to take the initiative.'

So: get rid of the templates. Question traditions. Find your own formats. Reach even more people.
Like before.

Is it possible that Igor's about to bring his active concert career to an end?

'That would make me very sad', Kristin Schuster says. 'I got to know him as one of the most fascinating artists of the present day – it would a shame if as many people as possible couldn't go on hearing that. If one day that's all gone, sharing things with a live audience, giving those concerts, if he says I'm tired, I've had enough: then I'll be the first person to say hey, then do something else. But I haven't had a sense of that yet. Sure, he sometimes seems exhausted, as we all do. But not in terms of what really matters: the connect between an artist and the audience – and the energy that flows there.'

'I think he also just wants to play', Simon Bode says. 'There are a lot of pieces where he says: it's so awesome that I can do that at last. I think he wants to enjoy that a bit too. We always forget how young he is.'

And Igor?

'Listen up', Igor says. 'I've got a joke for you. Herr Grün asks Herr Blau: Tell me, why do we Jews always have to answer questions with another question? And Blau says: Why not?'

The story might end like that. But it doesn't end as harmoniously as that.

\#

'Is hatred human?' Michel Friedman asks on the stage of the Berliner Ensemble on the Schiffbauerdamm on 29 September 2020. Igor replies: 'Yes, what else?'

He is a guest on the talk series 'Friedman in Conversation'. In the same setting, the host has already talked to German Foreign Minister Joschka Fischer about Europe, with the author Juli Zeh about home, and Cardinal Reinhard Marx about faith. This evening's theme, in black writing on a yellow background, is projected on the back wall of the stage: 'Hatred!'

Friedman is a lawyer, a television presenter and one of the most rhetorically brilliant minds in the country. He once belonged to the CDU national committee, and after that he was deputy chairman of the Central Council of the Jews in Germany. A person, then, who came to prominence for a reason other than his religion, but who in the context of several controversies and scandals seemed for many people to be reduced to a single attribute: Michel Friedman, the Jew.

It is curious that on this particular evening he of all people should be the one talking to Igor about hatred, because Friedman is probably the only person in the room to whom Igor doesn't need to explain himself on the subject. Friedman knows Igor's situation only too well from his own experience, since he has already taken the journey that Igor is travelling. So Friedman is facing Igor on the stage not only as an interviewer but also as a friend, adviser and therapist.

The event is interesting above all in relation to the things that will happen in the days that follow. Two days later Igor is due to be awarded the Order of Merit of the Federal Republic of Germany in Bellevue Palace, for the house concerts, which were seen as almost healing acts during the first Covid wave. But above all for his stand against anti-Semitism and other forms of hatred.

The reactions to the award were much less enlightening than might have been imagined in the context of such a subject. Critical and cynical voices mingled with the applause and congratulations. One prominent classical journalist fired a broadside against Igor: with his free streams he had ensured that music was being devalued. His Beethoven interpretations were mannered; he presented himself as an outsider, but he had long been part of the establishment; he put himself forward as a morally impeccable artist, when in fact his positions – against anti-Semitism and hateful anti-refugee policies – were far from remarkable, and in fact quite straightforward. And: he saw himself as a representative of less privileged artists, who in fact wanted none of it.

Igor didn't react.

One less prominent colleague said Igor's success was at the cost of all other musicians, because he took attention away from them.

Alice Weidel, chair of the AfD parliamentary faction, wrote an open letter to the President: Igor's award was 'a slap in the face to all those award recipients who had actually done well by their country and by our society.'

From Igor: not a word.

'Do you feel hatred?' Friedman asks him in the Berliner Ensemble. 'No', Igor says. 'I'm often furious, and sometimes I feel contempt. The people I'm furious with are very close to me. I don't care about people I despise. I like contempt better than hatred. Hatred is a long way away.'

Last of all, nearly two weeks after the award of the Cross of the Order of Merit, an article was published in the arts section of the *Süddeutsche Zeitung*. The author was Helmut Mauró, the music critic who had been writing about Igor's concerts in Munich, and who voiced the opinion that Igor presented studied effects rather than showing genuine emotions.

This time the author declared that Igor's political commitment was just another pose – the criticism of anti-Semitism was merely an 'amusing hobby' based on a dubious 'ideology of victimhood', in the knowledge that the image of the politically committed pianist will bring him in lots of friends in the left-wing and ecological Twitter milieu. At the piano Igor was far inferior to other pianists, and his musical success was ultimately based above all on the attention that he won through his fight against anti-Semitism. In other words: Igor stage-managed himself as a politically committed world-class pianist, but he was neither one nor the other – and anyone who valued him anyway had fallen for his PR strategy.

In the evening, after the paper's editors received a reaction far more of rage than of approval, the senior editors rowed back. The editor-in-chief declared initially that he stood by the article and Igor should write a reply, but later the paper published an apology: many readers and also colleagues on the newspaper thought the article was anti-Semitic and denigrating to Igor, and that had not been the intention – 'the question of what and how we can learn from this case will continue to preoccupy us'.

It's not clear what this debate is really about.

A criticism of the decision of the President's office to award the Cross of the Order of Merit to Igor? An attempt to stoke an existing controversy on the back of a person who was not in fact especially assailable, in order to find a particular set of readers? The battle of a print medium against an opposing public on Twitter? Perhaps even the battle of the authorities against an artist whose success no longer depended on their benevolence alone? Or only a reviewer who couldn't bear a pianist establishing himself even though he had spent almost a decade denying that he had any talent?

For Igor there was something else at the centre of it.

Not only had a German critic stated in this article that the commitment of a Jewish pianist, himself subject to repeated threats, to combatting anti-Semitism was an 'amusing hobby'.

More than anything, he had taken it upon himself to deliver the crucial interpretation of Igor. He explained to him who he was supposed to be, and that he had no right to be who he thought he was.

'Every injury leaves a wound', Igor says on the stage of the Berliner Ensemble. 'No injury is too small, and none of these wounds will heal. I've never associated that with the concept of hatred, but always with the idea of someone picking up an eraser and saying to me: actually you don't exist.'

'That's interesting', Friedman says. 'In this country we have a phrase, a metaphor that we should maybe talk about for a moment: *Wehret den Anfängen*. Nip it in the bud.[1] What do you think that actually means?'

'I have a problem with that phrase', Igor says. 'First of all linguistically. Maybe I'm too much of an immigrant, but I do have a problem with the suggestion of militarism that the German phrase contains. The phrase has a tone that I don't like. And added to that, from the point of view of my personal experience: it's a phrase that's seen from the point of view of the perpetrators. There's always a certain social agreement about what it means; it comes up again and again at every opportunity. But the same thing doesn't apply to the victims. Every time I read something about myself that annoys me and a friend says to me, Igor, don't make a big deal of it – that's an impossible instance of "nip it in the bud".

'If someone writes something about me on Twitter that might be construed as anti-Semitic, then that hurts terribly. Sure, it might be somebody with only 200 followers

---

1 A translation of Ovid's 'Principiis obsta', 'resist the beginnings'. Used in German political discourse to mean that unacceptable utterances should be stamped out before they can gain currency. (Translator's note.)

– but it still hurts. And what happens? A cycle begins that's completely understandable, it's always the same. I hear people saying: Igor, don't react! Don't dignify him! Don't give him a platform, don't give him a stage, he doesn't deserve the attention. Let other people do that. I get all that, but at that moment I explode. Anybody's allowed to say whatever they like about me, but I'm not allowed to respond? So the phrase 'nip it in the bud' doesn't apply to me? Or does it only apply when the chair of the AfD talks about me, is he big enough for me to be allowed to react? I love with all my heart the people who advise me, and I know that from their perspective they're right. But I really have to be careful, or I start shaking.'

'Are they right?' Friedman asks and goes on: 'I would disagree. You can always explain the words "nip it in the bud" in an entirely banal, ordinary way: I hear something, so I have to react. And if I don't react a million times, then my system of coordinates changes. "Leave well alone" means: it might be a bit of hatred, a bit of destruction, but just leave it be. I might quote Victor Klemperer, and this works very well in the context; we're talking about a kind of spiritual arson here. Klemperer said: words can be like tiny doses of arsenic. They are swallowed down unnoticed. They don't seem to have any effect, and yet after a while the effect of the poison is there anyway.'

The audience applauds.

Igor says: 'What a repellent and misanthropic idea it is for people to think that just because you're well known you don't feel pain. You can take it. No, you can't. And in my rage I think: let's have a little retweet – and the guy collapses like a little house of cards. Can I tell you a little joke?

'Kohn can't sleep at night, so he wakes up his wife Sarah and he says: I owe Grün money.

How much?

Ten thousand.

When do you need to give it to him?

Tomorrow.

Have you got it?

No.

And then Sarah says: Hang on, I'll just give him a call.

She calls him. Grün! Kohn owes you money?

Yes.

Ten thousand?

Yes.

And he has to give it to you?

Yes.

He hasn't got it.

And she hangs up. Kohn is furious. Are you meschugge, what have you done? And Sarah says: Now I can't sleep either.'

Laughter.

'Sometimes', Igor says, 'I catch myself thinking: Ok, I can't sleep. I could make sure that you can't sleep either. But no, I don't do anything. And yet I need to return to the pain. I know that pain; I know a lot of people who suffer pain because it wasn't meant personally. And that actually just makes it all the more painful. That pain doesn't go away. I go to bed with it and I wake up with it.'

It's to be hoped that this isn't also part of the reason why Igor sounds the way he does.

But unfortunately that's not entirely certain.

#

Berlin, autumn 2020, a Friday evening. Igor plays a programme of Beethoven sonatas at the Philharmonie, including the Appassionata. The Beethoven cycle is his solo debut in the Grand Hall. As on previous evenings the recital is sold out, but because of Covid it is only sparsely filled. The concert is being livestreamed on the internet. As ever Igor throws himself into the music, but the notes sound cool and isolated, while the apocalypse at the end of the last movement disperses into the back rows.

Hard to imagine a finale with more power, greatness and energy right now.

Less than a quarter of an hour after the last note he calls.

– Did you see it?

– Yes.

– Listen, could we chat for ten minutes? I'm cycling home right now, without lights or a helmet, so if I land on my face at least you'll hear it happen.

– Erm, right, sure.

– Oh Christ, it's raining now too.

– How was the concert?

– Pretty good, I think. Still feels like being at home. I sit there on this huge stage and play as if I'm in my living room. There's no difference now.

– Well yeah, but the tone was a bit better.

– Incredibly funny, really. Incredibly funny. Shit, it's blocked up ahead.

– Where are you now?

– Unter den Linden, about to get to the Brandenburg Gate.

He says nothing for a moment.

– You feel very German, cycling along here. Really very German, do you know that?

– In a good way or a not good way?

– I'm not sure. Wait a second, I just need to text somebody.

The sound of his airstream comes down the line.

– Right, done, back. So, how far along are we with the book? How much have we got?

A few moments later he turns into his road, opens the front door, says, 'Right, I'm home, thank you!', puts his bike over his shoulder and carries it upstairs into his apartment.

– What are you going to do now?

– I don't know. You?

– No idea.

And so this is the appropriate closing image.

Not the final applause in the Philharmonie, as in other books about pianists.

But Igor, dashing through Berlin in the rain at night, without lights or a helmet, and feeling as he did in the concert just before. Free of fear.

Full of coincidence that he's going to get there unscathed.

And driven by the desire not to be alone along the way.

#

Afterword

Hamburg, a Saturday evening in October 2021; a year after the last chapter. Igor is sitting in his dressing room in the Laeiszhalle, the city's second-biggest concert hall after the Elbphilharmonie. The black shirt that he was wearing on stage just now hangs over the back of a chair beside him. He is distributing – out of kindness and because he guesses that he would only eat it all himself otherwise – chocolate to the people who come and visit him at the interval.

He has half the Preludes and Fugues by Dmitri Shostakovich behind him, and the other half still to come. Igor is tired; on stage just now he was bursting with energy; now he looks listless and dull. 'That's a lot of pieces', he says. 'Do you think anybody'd notice if I left a few out?'

In fact, the Preludes and Fugues should really have appeared earlier in this book. Igor was invited to play the piano cycle, quite different from the Beethoven piano sonatas, but equally sprawling and boundless, in March 2020 at the Heidelberg Spring Festival. The work could have formed a nice counterpoint with the Beethoven sonatas. The concert was cancelled, and now the works only appear in the Afterword.

Igor, in the dressing room at the Laeiszhalle, puts his feet up.

The thing with the counterpoint isn't the only plan that came to nothing on the journey from the first page to the last. Ultimately the story is only marginal to the initial idea; a lot of good intentions ran aground, and instead there have been all kinds of fateful coincidences, so that the story seems to come together all by itself in the end, with arcs of tension and plot twists that could never have been predicted a moment before they happened.

In retrospect there could have been much more pleasant periods in which to tell a few chapters from Igor's life, but probably not a better one.

We've met up to discuss how the story could be updated for the English edition.

What's happened since the last chapter? A lot of things. And yet apparently not that much. It was a year when one often had a sense that time was running not forwards but backwards.

A few weeks after the last chapter the number of Covid infections in Germany rose again, and in early November the government decreed another lockdown, which lasted over six months and put a lot of people's nerves on edge. The stages and concert halls stayed closed until long into the spring, and when they opened up again, only a fraction of the audience was allowed in. Even when the rest of life had got back to normal. A lot of artists felt forgotten, abandoned, ignored, much more than during the first wave a year before.

Igor didn't resume his house concerts.

He used every available opportunity to appear in front of an audience; there weren't many opportunities. Even in lockdown he announced that he didn't want to play any more concerts transmitted by livestream from an empty concert hall.

In the spring Igor deleted his Twitter account, more out of weariness than caution. He no longer felt like engaging in the debates that were constantly going round in circles, the increasingly sharp tone, the transparent manoeuvres of right-wing populists that kept appearing. A few weeks later he did reactivate it, but in a much more muted form.

The unknown bidder who bought the music for his *Vexations* performance put the sheets up for sale again. This time every single page was sold – and the amount donated to freelance musicians rose considerably.

Igor's friend, the composer Frederic Rzewski, died in June.

In August Igor was a guest at the Salzburg Festival. On the programme: Symphony No. 3 in E flat major Opus 55 by Ludwig van Beethoven, the *Eroica*, in the transcription by Franz Liszt.

In September his recording of Ronald Stevenson's Passacaglia appeared on an album along with the Preludes and Fugues of Dmitri Shostakovich. The premiere of the album was held in the hangar of the decommissioned Berlin airport of Tempelhof, in front of a handful of spectators at the venue – and hundreds watching by livestream.

In October Igor flew to the USA and gave a concert on Thomas Mann's grand piano at Mann's villa in Los Angeles, playing: the

Sonata Opus 111 by Ludwig van Beethoven, which plays a leading role in Mann's novel *Doctor Faustus*.

And in January 2022 Igor, back in the USA, gave his debut in the big auditorium at Carnegie Hall.

And with that, the most important loose ends of the story were tied up. Was that it? Yes. And no, of course not.

Of course the story could all be told again with reference to different events. Then it would seem more up to date, newer, more present.

But Igor would still be Igor. Restlessly self-contained, exhausted by his tirelessness, overloaded and overtaxed by his own talent.

In the course of the year he seems to have become quieter, and at the same time noisier, more focused on the one hand and more agitated on the other. In other words: he hasn't changed a bit.

Igor, in the dressing room of Laeiszhalle, talks about a concert he played not long ago; on the programme: four Beethoven sonatas. He played the first one, then the second, then he went to the dressing room, took off his shirt, lay down on the sofa and turned on the television. After a few minutes the organizer tapped nervously on the door and asked if everything was ok. Yes, thanks, Igor said.
When did he plan to come back on stage, the organizer wanted to know.
Why?, Igor asked. How long's the interval?
Well, the audience is sitting in the hall waiting, the organizer said.
Oh shit, is there no interval?, Igor asked.
No, sorry, because of Covid there isn't one.

Then Igor dashed on stage, putting his shirt back on along the way, explained to the audience what had happened and played the two remaining sonatas and an encore as if nothing had happened.

It was the first time Igor had expected an interval where there wasn't one.
Normally it's the other way round.

Igor laughs, looks at his watch; in ten minutes he has to be back on stage.

And here, shortly before the start of the second part of the Preludes and Fugues by Dmitri Shostakovich with the audience gradually streaming back into the concert hall, the book ends for a second time.

The applause at the end of the evening is long and frenetic. Igor bows and squints into the audience. It looks as if he's checking that people are actually sitting in front of him, but in fact he's only dazzled by the spotlights. You don't need to read more into things than they actually contain.

And of course it would never occur to him to leave something out.